"To Emancipate the Mind and Soul"

Storer College
1867-1955

Harpers Ferry Park Association
P.O. Box 197
Harpers Ferry, WV 25425
(304) 535-6881
hfha@earthlink.net
www.harpersferryhistory.org

Copyright © 2017 Harpers Ferry Park Association
P.O. Box 197
Harpers Ferry, WV 25425
(304) 535-6881
hfha@earthlink.net
www.harpersferryhistory.org

Catherine Baldau, Editor
David T. Gilbert, Graphic Designer

The Harpers Ferry Park Association is a non-profit cooperating association supporting the educational and interpretive programs of Harpers Ferry National Historical Park. All proceeds from the sale of this publication benefit National Park Service programs.

ISBN: 978-0-9674033-3-5

Library of Congress Control Number: 2017909186

Front cover: Storer College graduating class of 1923, *West Virginia and Regional History Center, Storer College Digital College, West Virginia University*; Stained glass window from the Storer College Room, Stephen T. Mather Training Center (former Anthony Memorial Hall), *photo by Eric Long*.

Back Cover: Postcard, students and faculty in front of Lincoln Hall, ca. 1912, *Harpers Ferry National Historical Park Museum Collection*; Storer sweater, pennant, and beanie, *Harpers Ferry National Historical Park Museum Collection, photo by Eric Long*.

Dedication

For over forty years, Guinevere Roper has been a dedicated and loyal employee of Harpers Ferry National Historical Park. Through all of those years, her love and her passion has been the rich history of Storer College. Gwenny shared that passion far and wide and because of her, Storer College became the passion of others. She did groundbreaking research, shepherded the first park exhibit, developed the first Storer ranger programs, and provided unwavering support over the years to the college alumni. This book is dedicated to Gwenny, a tireless advocate whose contributions, love, and commitment will never be forgotten.

Acknowledgments

The Harpers Ferry Park Association extends its deepest appreciation to all those who made this publication possible. First and foremost, thank you to all of the contributors who embraced the idea of this project and gladly and enthusiastically gave us their time and talent.

It all began with the research, so we are indebted to Museum Specialist Michelle Hammer who readied the archives of Harpers Ferry National Historical Park and offered her assistance with research requests. Thank you also to George Best, who assisted in the archives and spent countless hours scanning historic photographs from the museum collection.

Sincere gratitude goes to David Fox, for his superlative editing and interpretive skills, and Autumn Cook, whose eye for detail and dogged search for the truth enriched this volume. Thank you to Jessica Eichlin and John Cuthbert at the West Virginia and Regional History Center at West Virginia University for their help accessing the Storer College Digital Image Collection, and to Guinevere Roper and Creighton Waters for their time spent combing through the WVU images. Thanks to Cynthia Gayton for her diligent Lovett family research and infectious passion for the subject, and to Norma Cole for her family stories and support. We are extremely grateful to Catherine Oliver, James Koenig, Annette Keener-Farley, and Andrea Gilbert for their invaluable editorial assistance.

Many thanks to David Gilbert, writer, editor, and graphic designer, for once again sharing his talent with the association. His outstanding publications have graced the shelves of the Park Bookshop for many years, and we are thrilled to add another to his distinguished list.

To Whitney Richards, Katlyn Simmons, Jennie Barnard, and Catherine Oliver, the staff of the association, whose teamwork upstairs and down allowed this project to happen. Special thanks to Susan Baker, whose spirit and smile keep us going, and Debbie Piscitelli, whose continued support of this organization inspires us daily to carry on her good work.

Finally, to all the staff of Harpers Ferry National Historical Park, those on the front lines and behind the scenes, the ones who wear the green and gray, thank you for being dedicated stewards of this public land, for protecting it, and for keeping the story of Harpers Ferry alive for generations to come.

Contents

Photo Credits

This volume is produced in partnership with the West Virginia and Regional History Center, West Virginia University Libraries. For additional Storer College images please visit: *https://storercollege.lib.wvu.edu*

Harpers Ferry National Historical Park, Historic Photo Collection: 22, 32, 33, 43, 59, 65, 67, 69, 70, 77, 79, 84, 87, 89, 95, 98, 131, 135, 137, 139, 149

Harpers Ferry National Historical Park, Museum Collection: 13, 21, 22, 35, 45, 117, 157 top, 158 top

Images from the *Free Baptist Cyclopaedia* (Chicago, 1889) in the Museum Collection: 38, 50, 53

Library of Congress, Prints and Photographs Online Catalog: 16, 17, 25, 26, 27, 39, 55, 71, 81, 97, 99

West Virginia and Regional History Center, Storer College Digital Collection, West Virginia University: 9, 10, 12, 15, 19, 20, 23, 41, 47, 58, 60, 63, 66, 83, 85, 86, 93, 100, 103, 107, 108, 109, 113, 118, 119, 122, 123, 127, 128, 130, 133, 143, 144, 145, 147, 157 bottom, 158 bottom, 159

Images from private collections are credited in the captions.

The ornaments than appear throughout these pages were originally printed in the *Storer College Sentinel*, 1909-1910.

*"Of all the civil rights for which the world has struggled
and fought for 5,000 years, the right to learn is undoubtedly
the most fundamental."*

—W. E. B. Du Bois

View of campus looking north. The stone building just to the right of center is the Lewis W. Anthony Building and beyond it is Anthony Memorial Hall with its distinctive cupola. This photo was taken between 1905, when the Lewis W. Anthony Building was constructed and 1911, when a water tower was erected behind Anthony Memorial Hall.

Introduction

When Elbert Norton returns to Harpers Ferry, time stands still. He is one of a dwindling number, the few remaining alumni of Storer College. Every summer, those who are able to travel meet for an alumni reunion at the former campus, now part of Harpers Ferry National Historical Park. "When I go back there, it seems my mind just opens up to a place," Elbert said in a recent interview. "I just come alive, just by seeing a difference in the mountains.... It seems like it renews my life."

Born in 1933, in segregated Alexandria, Virginia, just outside of Washington, DC, Elbert learned of Storer College from his neighbor. Ardelia Hunter, a Storer graduate who became an elementary school teacher and principal, encouraged Elbert to attend. "I saw the mountains, and I liked the scene," he recalls. "Once I got there, I didn't want to go anywhere else."

Elbert arrived on campus in the fall of 1951. He lived in Mosher Hall, majored in biology, sang in the school choir, played basketball, and attended mandatory vespers every Sunday at four o'clock. He met Mary Catherine Jackson at choir practice. When she scolded him for singing the wrong note, he asked if he could walk her home. She said yes. Six years later, they married in the Curtis Freewill Baptist Church, the same place he attended vespers every Sunday. Their reception was held in Cook Hall, a campus building. Elbert's class had the distinction of being the last to graduate from Storer College. Though six decades have passed, the school's 1955 closing still saddens Elbert. "I don't have a school to go back to...but...then again, I have been a part of history."

Elbert's future wife and her sister Margaret were in a different class of Storer's history—students who had to finish their education at another school. Like many students, Catherine and Margaret transferred to Shepherd College (now Shepherd University). Elbert believes the education they received at Storer prepared them well to transfer. "The kids that left Storer College during that time, they had no problem getting into any other school.... Virginia Union, West Virginia State, Morgan State, North Carolina A & T. They went everywhere, and most of them that I know they finished at other schools."

Catherine and Margaret were born a year apart in Halltown, West Virginia. The Jackson family moved to Bolivar then finally Harpers Ferry, where the children grew up in Storer's backyard. As a little girl attending Grandview Elementary School, Margaret brought popcorn to watch movies in Anthony Hall, went sled riding down Washington Street, and hunted for Easter eggs on the Storer lawn. As a Storer student, she attended dances on Friday and Saturday nights in the basement of Brackett Hall. In between classes she enjoyed chips and soda while listening to the jukebox in the PX. On the weekends she worked as a cleaner in the Bird-Brady House, where some of the female professors lived. Margaret also worked in the John Brown's Fort Museum, collecting the ten cent admission and selling souvenirs.

"Storer," Margaret remembers, "was an integral part of our life."

Margaret's mother, Mary Jackson, was the head cook in Brackett Hall. "I used to help my mother prepare food for the students," Margaret says, "especially early morning, because even though I had eight o'clock classes, I would get up with her at five and help her fix breakfast."

Like her sister, Margaret met her future husband at Storer College. Ulysses E. Smelley worked in Margaret's mother's kitchen as a dishwasher. Margaret wasn't impressed with Ulysses at first. "And then I found out he could sing, and he was a crooner, too." Margaret played the piano for him while he sang in the school talent shows. They married in 1957.

Margaret Jackson Smelley still remembers the day the trustees made the decision to close the college. "They had a meeting in the library.... They just came out and said, 'This is it. This is the last year.'" Though decades have passed, the image remains with her. "I remember them coming out with all of these long faces. That's when I knew the death knell had been struck."

The transfer to Shepherd College, just twelve miles from Harpers Ferry, proved challenging to Margaret. "One winter they had a cold room in McMurran Hall, and our music teacher took us across the street to get some coffee or tea.... The [restau-

Photo of an early spring gathering on the front lawn of Anthony Memorial Hall, Arbor Day, 1947. The somber appearance of the assembled and formal academic gowns worn by two participants suggest it may be a memorial planting.

Anthony Memorial Hall as pictured in the 1913-14 college catalogue. This former armory super-intendent's residence became the center of campus life at Storer College.

rant] owner told him that he could serve the rest of the students, but he couldn't serve us.… I wasn't used to that because at Harpers Ferry, we could go sit down wherever." Margaret encouraged the rest of the students to follow her out of the restaurant. "I proceeded to let it be known that I didn't appreciate it."

The atmosphere at Shepherd wasn't the same as her former school. "We were used to being embraced at Storer," Margaret says. She spent most of the school day at Shepherd sitting in a car "because you didn't have anywhere else to go. They didn't offer us a room or anywhere to sit. In between classes, we sat in our car." But Margaret persevered. She graduated from Shepherd College in 1957 with a BA in elementary education. "We didn't go there to get embraced. We went there to get an education. So we got that little piece of paper and left."

Returning to Harpers Ferry for Storer alumni reunions stirs more than memories for Margaret. Sitting on a bench, she thinks about running up and down the hill, the things she did on campus, the scar on the back of her leg she got when she tried to jump over a hedge. And she can't help but think of "what could have been."

Perhaps *what could have been* bears more weight because of *what was*. For eighty-eight years, Storer College was a school and sanctuary for African Americans free of bondage but still faced with innumerable and unfathomable challenges. From Reconstruction through the Civil Rights era—through the sheer will of the school's teachers, administrators, students, and benefactors from afar—this institution survived and thrived, providing an education for those previously denied the right to learn.

The story of Storer College began shortly after the Civil War ended, in an abandoned house wrecked by "shot and shell." Here a Freewill Baptist minister, a witness to the recent horrors of the battlefield, opened a school for newly freed slaves. His teachers, young female missionaries from the North, faced ridicule, slander, and the threat of physical violence from local whites still bitter in their defeat. Their students, coming from the "cradle of slavery to the throne of freedom" were eager to learn, one arriving with straw for the teachers who had no beds.

As the school expanded, so did the demand for teachers. In a midnight deal, a Maine philanthropist became a benefactor to this newly freed race. In October 1867, the freedmen's school became a "normal school" or teachers college. Their mission inspired religious women in the North. Most never set foot on the campus, yet they worked tirelessly to raise funds to pay for teachers, classroom materials, and buildings.

The leaders of the school were unwavering in their dedication to the school. Their first president secured buildings and land and helped African Americans find homes to establish a true college community. His successor served for forty-four years, committed "to emancipate the mind and soul" until his age and patriarchal views disconnected him from his students. For the school's first African American president, a burning cross in his yard did not deter him from his crusade to make Storer College the best school he could for the student body.

Storer produced a distinguished roster of alumni: The first black attorney in West Virginia who helped found a civil rights organization. A woman born into slavery, with an extraordinary gift for elocution, who became an educator, speaker, and leader in the civil rights and women's suffrage movements. One diminutive musical prodigy became known as "The Little Giant of Jazz." Another student went on to become a preeminent scientist before returning to his alma mater to teach. And there is the African boy who excelled at academics and sports and later became the first president of the Federal Republic of Nigeria.

October 2017 marks the 150th anniversary of the founding of this historically black college. To honor this occasion, Harpers Ferry Park Association, in partnership with Harpers Ferry National Historical Park, invited park rangers, professors, journalists, students, and scholars to help tell the story of the people who lived, learned, and worked on the "hill of hope." Their collaborative effort reveals tales of courage and conviction, success and defeat, controversy, and, above all, hope.

Though much research has been done over the past year, there are troves of Storer College stories yet to be unearthed. Researchers continue to discover primary sources, uncovering former facts as inaccurate. As mysteries are solved, new ones arise. This volume does not aim to be a complete scholarly resource but rather an accessible anthology that allows the reader a glimpse into an extraordinary, little-known piece of American history.

A Brief History

By James Koenig

"The estimated colored population in Harpers Ferry is five hundred, an estimate which seems to me too low…. If something is not done soon for their relief, they may well despair…. At (Harpers Ferry) there is one day school with forty two pupils." —From an 1867 field report sent to the Freedmen's Bureau, Washington, DC

That "one day school" in post-Civil War Harpers Ferry, opened by Freewill Baptist missionaries in a borrowed, war-damaged building, soon became Storer College, one of the first institutes of higher learning open to all regardless of sex, race, or religion. For almost ninety years, Storer provided remedial education, teacher training, and academic studies to anyone willing to learn—though African Americans were the primary intended students.

The fact that Storer College existed is nothing short of a miracle. Teaching a disadvantaged population that for hundreds of years had been denied educational opportunities was a daily struggle. From the very first imaginings of the school until it was

Campus view of Anthony Memorial Hall (right), Brackett Hall (center), and John Brown's Fort (left), used to house a museum. In the foreground can be seen chalk lines of the football field and in the background, peeking out above the roof of Anthony Memorial Hall, is a water storage tower, erected in 1915. In the early twentieth century, Storer built its own central water supply system prompting the college president to declare indoor plumbing "one of the greatest blessings we have ever had."

permanently shuttered, the Storer saga was always characterized by seemingly insurmountable odds—and the brave, heroic figures who consistently defied them. From 1867 to 1955, Storer College stood on the "hill of hope," a testament to the courage, faith, and fortitude of those who studied, taught, dreamed, and otherwise invested themselves in the school's community.

The War Winds Down: Education Begins in Harpers Ferry

Between 1864 and 1865, the Union army attempted to provide schooling to the contraband slaves who had streamed into Harpers Ferry. Major General Franz Sigel, a former New York City schoolteacher, granted rations, quarters, and classroom materials to W.W. and Ellen Wheeler of the Protestant-based American Missionary Association to operate a freedmen's school. Though short-lived, records indicate the Wheelers provided instruction to fifty to sixty pupils in both day and night classes.

By several estimates, the combined population of slaves and freedmen in the Harpers Ferry area at war's end was around seven hundred, more than double the pre-war population. The influx of refugees and those freedmen already in residence suffered not only from malnutrition, disease and poverty, but had difficulty finding housing and work. An eyewitness reported that in 1865 the area known as Camp Hill on the heights above Harpers Ferry "was literally swarming with colored people." This situation exacerbated the simmering animosity a majority of the white population had for African Americans in Harpers Ferry and the surrounding area.

A James E. Taylor sketch of Lockwood House in 1864 while used as headquarters by Gen. Philip Sheridan. Damaged by fighting and neglect, this building soon became classroom, dormitory, church, and haven for newly freed slaves and their teachers.

Throughout the Civil War, runaway slaves, known as contraband, sought refuge by following the Union army north. This July 1865 photo by James Gardner shows the ruins of the U.S. Armory next to the Potomac River and scattered, makeshift tents used for contraband housing.

The impending freedom of four million slaves was a looming crisis of immense proportion. Northern religious groups rightly perceived that education was a fundamental key to long-lasting improvement of the lives of former slaves. Their movement to provide education to freedmen was viewed as both a means of self-improvement and a way to spread the Christian faith. The missionaries who came south to establish schools quickly realized that an estimated twenty thousand teachers would be needed when full emancipation came at war's end—a number their own ranks could not fill. Many believed the most effective strategy would be to train African Americans to become teachers. To face this monumental challenge, religious groups began earnest fundraising, initially supplying their own administrators and teachers. Within a few short years, eleven colleges were founded, along with sixty-one "normal schools" created specifically for training teachers.

One religious group to focus on Harpers Ferry—and the one important to the founding of Storer—was a New England-based, largely white denomination, the Freewill Baptists (synonymously known in its history as Free Will Baptists and Free Baptists). In 1865, Freewill Baptists were actively establishing freedmen schools and churches in the Shenandoah Valley, including four loosely connected towns in the Eastern Panhandle of West Virginia: Harpers Ferry, Charles Town, Shepherdstown, and Martinsburg. Eventually, Harpers Ferry became the primary focus for their considerable efforts.

On November 25, 1865, a little over six months after the war ended, Freewill Baptists opened a primary school in Harpers Ferry. Classes were held in the abandoned Lockwood House, which had once been the armory paymaster's house, then a wartime hospital and headquarters. Attendance sometimes exceeded one hundred students of various ages for day and evening classes. From the start, teachers confronted the educational and social disadvantages of formerly enslaved African Americans that had persisted for the previous 250 years. Most freedmen could not read, write, or do arithmetic; their verbal skills were rudimentary at best; hygienic practices were new to many; infant mortality was extremely high, and they were vulnerable to disease. While focusing instruction on the basics of spelling, reading, language, and arithmetic, these early teachers also faced the bitter, sometimes violent contempt of white Southerners still affected by their losses suffered in the Civil War. Knowing the immensity of the task before them, the Freewill Baptists were not deterred.

Storer College Opens

Like other groups, Freewill Baptists decided to direct most of their missionary outreach to establishing a normal school for training teachers in Harpers Ferry. Through the generous bequest of Maine philanthropist John Storer and the fundraising efforts of the Freewill Baptists, combined with sizeable grants from the federal government, the college opened in October 1867. They taught in the same government building, the Lockwood House, which had been used for the freedmen's school. Seventeen pupils were reported in attendance. From the beginning, room and board were offered to incoming students, though the conditions were primitive at best. Overcrowding was endemic, and the scramble to create makeshift dormitories would be an enduring challenge over the decades.

Though it was a start, the Freewill Baptists did not own the Lockwood House or the three other nearby government buildings that they needed for expected growth in attendance. They continued lobbying the federal government, and in 1868, Congress granted them the four buildings free of charge. The three other buildings soon became known as Brackett House, Morrell House, and Anthony Hall (also called Anthony Memorial Hall). Having been abandoned at the start of the war, damaged during the fighting, and left open to weather, all four buildings were in lamentable disrepair.

Given the devastation and shortage of funds, even these seemingly uninhabitable buildings were a welcome start. Soon enough, three of the four buildings were fully utilized even as repairs were slowly being made. The buildings were used variously as living quarters for the families of administrators and teachers, student dorms, classrooms, offices, and anything else that needed space, including a chapel. Use of Anthony Hall would be postponed until local resentment toward the college had died down.

With enrollment climbing to 160 in 1870, the future looked promising. However, pupils often needed remedial schooling before they could advance, so one of the academic divisions was Preparatory. The other two were State Normal and Academic. Of note, Storer was the only institution in West Virginia offering higher education to African Americans until nearly the end of the nineteenth century.

Students posing for a graduating class photo in 1895.

By 1890, it was estimated that over 500 teachers received part or all of their training at Storer. These teachers fanned out into West Virginia and the surrounding states teaching African American children in schools then segregated by law.

Heartened with their modest success, school administrators, teachers, and supporters would soon be tested to the limit dealing with a multiplicity of tasks ahead of them. Just a few of these included: curriculum development; recruitment of teachers, staff and students; acquisition of property for investment or campus expansion; renovation of existing buildings; building or acquiring additional buildings, facilities and grounds; day-to-day maintenance of buildings and grounds; outfitting classrooms; managing student housing and dining facilities; regulating student life; attending to student health issues; public relations; on-going fundraising; and so on and on. Literally anything and everything needed to grow and sustain a college community had to be addressed, from the mundane task of clearing snow from sidewalks, to steering through crises like the influenza epidemic of 1918.

Student Life

From the beginning, every aspect of student life was regulated according to Christian principles for moral behavior and what college administrators believed necessary

Storer choir singing as they exit Curtis Freewill Baptist Church, ca. 1920.

to ensure academic success. Rest and study periods were strictly monitored, as well as class attendance. Students could not leave campus without permission, and a specific code of rules and prohibitions governed interaction with the opposite sex. Female students received even closer scrutiny and were not allowed out after dark or allowed to go to the train station unescorted. Fancy or provocative dress by either sex was not permitted. Church attendance was mandatory, though students were allowed to go to a church of their own choice or of their parents choosing.

While the regulations and prohibitions were stringent by today's standards, they were on par with other colleges' requirements of student behavior. Much later, as social mores changed and awareness of African American rights increased, there were reports of student "restiveness." Like most colleges even through the 1960s, rebellious students were quickly expelled and those associated with them punished in lesser ways.

One of the most intangible but most important aspects of college life at Storer was the sense of community it fostered. In many ways it was a place of refuge from a wider world rife with racial prejudice. This sense of community was clearly seen in the strength and loyalty of the alumni association, and the enthusiasm still shown by alumni today. The college newspaper, the *Storer Record*, featured news from alumni, reporting on job changes, family news, deaths, and fond recollections of college life. The paper also noted visits of alumni to the campus that seemed to be a weekly occurrence throughout the school year. As one former student put it, "Here you will gain new understanding of community living and of friendships."

Challenges at Every Turn

It took immense effort to open, grow, and sustain Storer for eighty-eight years. One on-going impediment was a cumbersome governing board that was slow to act and often ignored requests for direction. By default, administrators were often left to act on important matters without authority to do so. On top of that, the Storer College Board of Trustees refused any request that might result in the accrual of debt. The

*View of students and instructor, William Peregoy (left), in the carpentry shop classroom, ca. 1907.
Students are dressed for class with ties tucked safely inside aprons. The presence of a room heating
stove indicates that central heating had not yet been installed.*

board's spotty oversight and adherence to a "pay as you go" policy often hampered the
arduous effort to build and maintain a campus. Through dedicated leadership and the
early fundraising support of alumni and the Freewill Baptists, Storer was able survive
and grow.

Throughout the second half of the nineteenth century and into the early twentieth century the college acquired property and buildings and built new facilities such
as Lincoln Hall, a dormitory for men, and Myrtle Hall, a dormitory for women. After
extensive renovations and significant enlargement, Chapel Hall (the former armory
superintendent's house) was renamed Anthony Memorial Hall and eventually became
the center of campus life. That left three of the original buildings—Lockwood, Brackett, and Morrell—on the far eastern side of the campus. The college periodically considered selling the buildings but kept them as backup dorms or overflow classroom
space given the unpredictable size of student population from year to year.

By 1915, the college had seventeen buildings, up from eight in 1906. Imagine the
challenge to renovate each of these buildings to accommodate the successive modern
milestones of central heating, electric lighting, and indoor plumbing introduced by the
first quarter of the twentieth century. Modernization extended to the campus grounds
included lighting, improved sidewalks, and hard surface roads and parking areas. Unless a shortcut was taken, mud was no longer an ever-present problem when walking
to classes or the dining hall.

The expansion and revitalization of the campus and buildings was due to the leadership of Henry T. McDonald, who had become college president in 1899. When he arrived on campus, he couldn't help but notice that the buildings and grounds had grown shabby and the curriculum outdated. It was difficult to hire and retain new teachers, leaving a dearth of qualified instructors. The board would not support an increase in wages to make Storer competitive with other colleges, so low salaries hampered recruitment. Teachers without much experience were attracted to Storer as their stepping stone to career advancement. Even with the offer of free housing, board, and electric as incentives, teacher retention did not improve.

Once the campus and buildings were spruced up, classrooms modernized, curriculum updated and expanded, and more teachers hired, it was hoped that student enrollment would increase. That did not happen on a consistent basis, putting the college in a continual financial bind. In 1900, there were 146 students, down from 237 in 1884. Only eighty students were enrolled in 1905. Sometimes enrollment did increase but was never sustained. This made it very difficult to plan for student housing from year to year, not to mention anticipating income and how many faculty members would be needed.

Some of the specific factors for declining enrollment included: induction into military service for large numbers of young African Americans in World Wars I and II; from 1929 to 1941 the Great Depression made paying for advanced schooling a luxury few African American families could afford; and the state of West Virginia opened two state normal schools exclusively for African Americans in direct competition with Storer. And, with the opening of these schools, state funding for Storer, always meager, was cut even further.

In 1921, Storer achieved junior college status and awarded it first associate degrees in 1923. The founding dream of the college to award four-year degrees was finally realized in 1939. They offered majors in five areas including two teaching certificates: elementary collegiate and standard normal.

Student enrollment did climb somewhat during the Depression years from 119 in 1933 to 171 in 1939. This was possible only through the fundraising efforts of the school's president, enabling financial aid to be provided to a significant number of students. Even with this fundraising success, Storer

A ca. 1920 postcard of a graduate posed in front of Anthony Memorial Hall.

One of the last images of students and faculty in front of Brackett Hall in 1953. Faced with declining enrollment and financial restraints, the school would close in just two years.

College experienced a twenty-five percent salary cut for faculty and staff. By 1940, just when things were starting to look up for the national economy, WWII began. Student enrollment plummeted to eighty-two—nearly all women. It dropped even further to a low of forty-four as the war dragged on. However, once the war ended there was a dramatic increase of students because of educational benefits provided under the G.I. Bill. By the late 1940s, this surge tapered off, and enrollment barely justified keeping the college open.

A Proud Institution Finally Closes

The fortunes of the college were clearly on the decline after the initial surge of enrollment following the end of WWII. It was clear to all that Storer could not continue the same way it had. In an apparent nod to changing times, the board hired Dr. Richard I. McKinney as Storer's first African American president in 1944. Given his academic credentials and standing in the African American community, there was reason to hope his hiring might turn things around. But, relations with the board and some supporters quickly soured, and many in the local community weren't pleased to have an African American lead the college. Dr. McKinney's vision for the college was progressive, even daring for the times, such as recruiting more African American teachers, establishing a chapter of the NAACP on campus, giving students a greater voice in college affairs, and strengthening ties with the African continent. These initiatives and others were usually met with disfavor and, sometimes, outright opposition from board members, alumni, and the local community.

As Dr. McKinney rightly sensed, times were changing, and the college needed to be on the forefront of promoting social change and civil rights. But he was obviously ahead of the times and offered his resignation in 1949. (The board waited until 1950 to accept it.) Setting aside his controversial agenda for the college, it is unlikely Dr. McKinney would have been successful given the dire state of the college's finances.

There were attempts to reverse the school's fortunes. One plan called for Storer to become a state school, but internal politics and legislative maneuvers eventually killed it. Another was to find wealthy benefactors to support the school, but that attempt also failed.

Some attribute the school's closing to *Brown v. Board of Education*, in which the Supreme Court ended the "separate but equal" doctrine for schools. The 1954 ruling likely weighed heavily on the board's decision to finally close the school in 1955. The Supreme Court's decision prompted the state legislature to end even the pittance it was giving Storer because African Americans by law could now attend any school in West Virginia. This, combined with other factors, including low enrollment and an ever-aging physical plant, meant there was no saving the college.

The Legacy of Storer College

The founders started a school with a straightforward mission: to provide an education to former slaves and Freemen and their descendants. By any measure they succeeded reaching that goal. For twenty-five years Storer College was the only school in West Virginia where any person of color could get an education beyond the primary level. The early initiative to train greatly multiplied the educational opportunities for African Americans in West Virginia and the surrounding states. In addition to their educational advantage, those who attended Storer migrated across the country, serving as positive role models in their communities.

In a quiet though important way, the success of Storer symbolized something not seen very often today. The founders, successive administrators, staff, and teachers were the epitome of selflessness, personifying a willingness to sacrifice for the benefit of mankind. They were the embodiment of the Storer College motto:

Labor Omnia Vincit
(*Work Conquers All*)

CHAPTER 1

Freewill Baptists and the Freedmen's Bureau, 1865-1868

By Matt Coletti

By 1863, the American Civil War was at its zenith. Despite the long road to victory that still lay ahead, military and political leaders in Washington began formulating a strategy to reconstruct the southern United States. Among the most pressing matters addressed within their strategy was the fate of former slaves in the postwar South. The War Department quickly put a plan of action into place. Its policies established the American Freedmen's Inquiry Commission, which in turn, devised an agency known as the "Bureau of Freedmen, Refugees, and Abandoned Lands," otherwise simply called the "Freedmen's Bureau." While the Bureau cared for southern white refugees and administered abandoned Confederate property, its primary concern was the wellbeing of newly emancipated slaves. General Oliver Otis Howard, a Union war hero and abolitionist, helmed the agency, which provided temporary civil services to help the new freedpeople.

In July 1865, Freedmen's Bureau branches popped up throughout the occupied South, aiding black communities as part of the federal government's gargantuan effort to reconstruct the region. Although Jefferson County had controversially joined the southern Union state of West Virginia during the war, it, too, received attention from the Freedmen's Bureau. On the eve of the conflict, some five thousand enslaved African Americans lived in Jefferson County. Many more fled down the Shenandoah Valley, seeking refuge with the Union army that was periodically at Harpers Ferry. By the war's end, military officials noticed the deteriorating living conditions among local African Americans, and a branch of the Freedmen's Bureau opened that month in response. Several junior army officers

Gen. Oliver O. Howard, leader of the Freedmen's Bureau and namesake of Howard University, a historically black university founded in 1867. Gen. Howard served as its president from 1869 to 1874.

ran the post, including Captains W. Stover Howe, George W. Wells, and John C. Burbanker. A few of them, like the outspoken Lieutenant Augustus F. Higgs, fought in some of the war's fiercest engagements. But all were firmly wedded to the Freedmen's Bureau. The officers unfortunately never had the support of a permanent garrison, which greatly handicapped their ability to do their job. To tackle such an obstacle,

The schoolhouses in the South established by the Freedmen's Bureau and Northern Missionaries were typically in rough, poorly-fitted buildings or cabins, such as this one at Edisto Island, South Carolina.

the supervisors sought assistance from concerned civilians, white and black, as well as likeminded public servants.

The foremost among those allies to the local Freedmen's Bureau were the Freewill Baptists, led in the Shenandoah Valley by Reverend Nathan Cook Brackett. They hailed from New England and were long committed to the cause of abolition. The reverend and his colleagues arrived in the Shenandoah Valley as part of the United States Christian Commission, helping civilians and soldiers of both sides during the Valley Campaigns of 1864. When the war ended, they saw the extreme plight of the freed people and offered relief. Together, the Freedmen's Bureau and the Freewill Baptists initiated a number of welfare programs for former slaves. Bureau agents and Freewill Baptist missionaries engaged in activities that ranged from legal mediation to the monitoring of labor contracts with white employers. Although black suffrage did not exist in Jefferson County until 1869, Freewill Baptists led by Brackett and local African Americans organized clandestine social clubs called "Union Leagues" to prepare the black community to vote.

The Freewill Baptists' most consequential impact manifested from their ability to produce educational opportunities. Their influence helped construct and maintain sixteen African American public schools in all the major towns of Jefferson County at a cost of more than $4,500. At first, the Bureau allowed the Freewill Baptists to administer the schools but removed their authority in 1866 by placing the facilities under the care of the county school boards. Still prominent, Brackett became the superintendent that same year, and the school boards relied heavily upon the Freewill Baptists for teachers, many of whom were young women. According to Bureau reports, adults and children eagerly participated, with some 350-400 students nightly attending a school created by Reverend Brackett himself. Buoyed by success, the Freedmen's Bureau and the Freewill Baptists undertook the creation of a "normal school" at Harpers Ferry in 1867.

Despite their accomplishments, many obstacles beleaguered the resources at the disposal of the Freedmen's Bureau and the Freewill Baptists. Although quite a few African Americans prospered in the first years after the war, agents and missionaries had difficulty supporting black financial stability in Jefferson County. Finding shelter for women, children, and the elderly proved a challenging task because rental rates set by whites were far too expensive. Outbreaks of smallpox and cholera in both 1866 and 1867 devastated the black community, compelling frantic medical coordination with local doctors.

The animosity of most whites to the changes induced by both organizations imposed the greatest burden of all for both the Freedmen's Bureau and the Freewill Baptists. Because whites in Jefferson County had largely backed the Confederacy, they were nearly united against the advancement of their black neighbors. Those whites constantly harassed the Bureau agents and Freewill Baptist missionaries, necessitating armed guards. County newspapers, like the *Spirit of Jefferson*, savagely slandered the

This Harper's Weekly *illustration shows a lone Freedmen's Bureau employee attempting to stop a riot between white southerners and African Americans. Congress created the Freedmen's Bureau in 1865 to help protect the rights of newly freed slaves in the South, but southern states found ways to circumvent the laws and impose restrictions on African Americans.*

Bureau and the Freewill Baptists as well. The *Spirit of Jefferson* even called Brackett and a fellow missionary "Massachusetts interlopers" who had the "short-sightedness of John Brown and his deluded followers" for aiding the freed people. Whites manning the school boards and law enforcement sabotaged both organizations at every opportunity by blocking black school funds and equal treatment in court.

The most aggressive outburst of this enmity occurred when a race riot exploded in Charles Town during July 1868. Over a hundred people clashed, prompting the officer in charge of the Bureau, Captain John C. Burbanker, to wire his Washington superiors for reinforcements to quell the violence: "Send us twenty men with a good officer immediately." When Burbanker recounted the incident in September, he indicated that more than a dozen people were injured in the fighting. Federal troops and local officials restored order a few days later and arrested some of the initial perpetrators regardless of their race. All received light sentences in the form of a fine.

The Freedmen's Bureau closed its small office in Harpers Ferry just before Ulysses S. Grant won his first presidential race in 1868. It was forced to halt activity in Jefferson County and turn all operations over to local oversight. The agency's bureaucrats had determined that the needs of African Americans throughout West Virginia were adequately addressed, despite evidence suggesting otherwise. Over the next few years, indifferent and hostile whites dominated the county government and overturned most of the positive changes introduced by the Bureau and the Freewill Baptists. One of those changes, however, survived the partnership's demise: the "normal school" that became Storer College.

CHAPTER 2

The Labor of a Free Man

By David Fox

H e thought they were going to kill him.

Barely a year after the Civil War ended, an angry mob of white people in Charles Town surrounded Nathan Brackett. They must have been fuming over the enormous cost of the war, and they seemed intent on crushing Brackett, a Yankee intruder who represented everything they hated. This was the town where John Brown and his men were hanged for slave insurrection in 1859. How dare Brackett organize a school for former slaves here!

Accepting defeat was a bitter pill for the Confederate side. This was still Virginia in their minds, not West Virginia, where it had been illegal to teach any person of color the alphabet. Their courthouse was burnt, their farms ruined, far too many of their young men were dead, and now this Yankee was trying to educate their former slaves.

Suddenly, a young man appeared and faced the crowd. He warned the mob that they would have to fight him if they harmed a hair on Brackett's head. As a Confederate soldier in 1864, this young man had been left for dead on the battlefield at Cedar Creek. Two days after the battle Brackett found him and saved his life. The mob backed down for a moment and the reverend slipped away.

Reverend Nathan Cook Brackett, born July 28, 1837, in Phillips, Maine, had been an agent for the United States Christian Commission during the last year of the war. He had tried to enlist in the army several times, but a chronic bronchial condition kept him from military ser-

Reverend Nathan Cook Brackett, ca. 1864. (Photo courtesy of Todd Bolton)

vice. After earning his degree from Dartmouth, his desire to serve led him to the Christian Commission. He said, "The thought that I was relieving suffering and doing good afforded me infinite happiness."

While serving the soldiers of the Union army in the Shenandoah Valley, Brackett made his way to and from the front, delivering mail, tending to the wounded, identifying the dead, and sending soldiers' pay home to their families. He said that he "was continuously in the midst of misery and suffering. I witnessed scores of heart-breaking scenes…. The surroundings were such as I should never care to witness again…. The stirring situation aroused me for my work and I learned never to shirk or hesitate." His supervisor said, "It was impossible to give [Brackett] too much to do."

The most dangerous part of Brackett's job was carrying soldiers' pay from Winchester to Harpers Ferry to be mailed home. He said, "The country was dotted with hostile foes and frequently by outlaws. I was not afraid of being robbed but my life was constantly in danger. At times I used to carry concealed about my person twenty thousand dollars. Of course I always had to have an escort and I had to watch my chances so as to go in the safest company and at the safest times. Fortunately I was never harmed on these journeys and never in all my transactions for the soldiers lost a dollar."

Five months after the war ended, Brackett returned to New England to continue his education as a Freewill Baptist minister. Church elders, however, convinced Brackett that his God-given mission was to educate the newly freed people in the Shenandoah Valley. Within one month, Brackett accepted a one-year appointment for the mission, married his sweetheart, Louise Wood, and returned to the Valley. He stayed for the rest of his life.

Brackett soon represented not only the Freewill Baptist Home Mission Society but also the American Missionary Association and the U.S. Freedmen's Bureau. All three agencies wanted him to be the superintendent of schools for the freed people. In 1865, there were 30,000 formerly enslaved people in the Shenandoah Valley searching for family members, work, and a place to learn. Many of them were streaming down the Valley toward Harpers Ferry. Louise Wood Brackett described the newly freed people as "a floating population, stranded on the sea of poverty." Nathan Brackett created a safe harbor, where the rising tide of education could lift all boats.

The U.S. Armory (or musket factory) at Harpers Ferry was destroyed when the war began, and the government did not restore it. That meant a lot of buildings were empty and potentially available. The abandoned federal houses on Camp Hill were well situated above the flood prone valleys, with panoramic views of the Blue Ridge Mountains. A journalist described these buildings as "relics of fine old mansions where bats reign supreme." At no charge, the U.S. Government allowed the Bracketts and four young teachers to live in the Lockwood House, although a sick and wounded army veteran and his family already occupied one of the rooms. Brackett described his new, old house with "naked and battered walls, only partially supplied with windows, and roof riddled by shells and cannon balls." Brackett and his new staff patched the cannonball holes in the roof and walls and replaced the missing windows and doors. For two years Lockwood House served as home, classroom, church, and dormitory.

Outside of their building, however, the teachers and their students could not have been more unwelcome. In Brackett's words, "We are having serious trouble just now—or our pupils are. The bloodhounds are all loose. They have attacked our evening scholars several times lately. Last night four of the men fought their way through quite a crowd. They are threatening to burn our house." New teachers were insulted and stoned in the streets by local whites, and the newspapers ridiculed and slandered them. Brackett said that this school "had its birth during the most intense and bitter period of…Reconstruction—the whole South was in a fever of excitement…. The period…was one of intense anxiety and labor."

A group of contraband slaves photographed in Harpers Ferry in front of the former U.S. Armory superintendent's house in 1862. After the war, Rev. Nathan Brackett helped negotiate the transfer of this property to Storer College, where African Americans would return to Harpers Ferry to receive a formal education. (Image from the Wingate History of 22nd NY State Militia)

The next year, Brackett pushed south up the Shenandoah Valley and set up schools in Berryville, Winchester, Front Royal, Woodstock, Harrisonburg, Staunton, and Lexington. Over two thousand students went to school for the first time in their lives.

By 1867, Brackett's small mission school in Harpers Ferry underwent a change that began to fulfill the Freewill Baptists' larger educational goals. Everyone involved in the mission knew that one-room elementary schools scattered across the Shenandoah Valley were just a beginning. The mission needed to grow with teachers from the African American community and opportunities for higher education. Brackett's school came to the attention of a wealthy Maine businessman, John Storer, who wanted to share his wealth and support Reconstruction and education. He challenged them to match a $10,000 donation. They succeeded, and in October 1867 Storer College was born.

Nathan Brackett soon went from principal of a tiny school to president of an institution of higher learning. The need for space and for more buildings to grow the school was obvious. In 1868, Congress passed a bill that transferred ownership of Lockwood House and three other buildings on Camp Hill to Storer College. Brackett must have been elated. However, the transfer was delayed one year by a dispute over the character of Brackett's students and the boundaries of the government property.

The dispute involved Daniel Young, a former armory official, who was the caretaker of all the government property at Harpers Ferry. He lived only a few blocks from Lockwood House. Brackett had recruited Young to serve on the Board of Trustees of Storer College. Unfortunately, what appeared to be a positive relationship turned sour. Faced with the pending property transfer, Young tried to stop it by sending scathing reports to the War Department insulting Brackett's students and condemning their behavior. He predicted that the government property would be devalued or even destroyed by students' fighting, drinking, and fireworks. Young's charges prompted an investigation by the Freedmen's Bureau, which concluded all charges were false.

Next, Young objected to the property line between the front yard of Lockwood House and the Harper Cemetery. He pored over the 1782 will of the town's founder, Robert Harper, and determined that the Harper Cemetery should expand to take over the Lockwood House front yard. Young argued that the beautifully landscaped, terraced two acres east of Lockwood did not belong in the land transfer to Storer College.

Brackett and Young presented dueling surveys and letters to government officials to make their opposing cases. In December 1869, the cemetery was enlarged to within 53 feet of Lockwood's front porch. Brackett's reaction to this setback may have been reflected in the words of another college official who called it "theft," and said, "Only an unjust court could have agreed to such a bare faced steal."

When the property transfer was finally completed, the school gained desperately needed room to expand, but lost two valuable acres that would soon be covered with tombstones. Ironically, perhaps, Nathan Brackett and his family were buried in this section of the Harper Cemetery.

Built as quarters for the armory superintendent's clerk, this building was one of the four original buildings that made up Storer College. The school's founder, Rev. Nathan Brackett lived here with his wife until his death in 1910.

Nathan and Louise Brackett (seated, on left, second row) ca. late 1870s. Brackett's sister Lura, a teacher from the Free Baptist Woman's Missionary Society, is seated on the far right.

Perhaps the lowest point in Brackett's tenure occurred in the 1890s. By this time Storer and its friends had carved out a place in the community. Brackett had helped over forty African Americans in town buy land and own houses, and most opposition to the school had faded from view. But a new source of hatred emerged from within the Storer College family. This opposition resulted from a decision affecting the tourism and summer boarding house business, which had become a fixture at Harpers Ferry. With the Board of Trustees approval, Brackett had been renting school buildings to approved proprietors, both black and white. Guests, black and white, from Washington and Baltimore often filled up six different buildings. Boarders commented on the excellent service provided by students who were not only making money to pay for school but also learning business skills. Brackett used the income to broker real estate deals and homeownership for staff and former students.

In 1896, the summer business in Lincoln Hall, the largest building for boarders, was a losing proposition. The Board of Trustees directed Brackett to shut it down. At the same time he was told to entertain offers to reopen or expand this business. It didn't matter when another building might open or who might rent it. It was too late. Jim Crow segregation was sweeping the land and Lincoln Hall had been the primary boarding house for African Americans. A protest meeting of "Alumni and friends" resulted in charges of racism against Brackett for ending summer boarding for African Americans on campus.

The "Alumni and friends" also called Brackett a "sad failure" as a teacher, accused him of mishandling finances, of hiring "old maids and old bachelors," and "having alienated the best ministers." A former student and current teacher, William Bell, was the most outspoken. He had lost money renting out Lincoln Hall, owed Brackett $450, and had a sharp disagreement with Brackett over financing a house for a colleague. Bell was also on the verge of losing his own house for defaulting on his mortgage.

Bell found a powerful ally in J. R. Clifford, a Storer graduate, West Virginia's first black attorney, and editor of the *Pioneer Press*. Clifford had been carrying a grudge against Brackett for fifteen years. Articles and editorials in the *Pioneer Press* written by Bell and Clifford slandered Brackett as "a leech and a thief." From 1896 to 1899, Clifford filed several lawsuits against Brackett over the same real estate financing that upset Bell. Clifford lost them all and had to pay court costs and judgments in each case.

At a campus church business meeting in 1897, Bell was summoned to face Brackett and settle their differences according to church bylaws. Bell never showed up. One month later, Bell was expelled from the Freewill Baptist Church "for having published matter of a malicious nature containing false statements in the Pioneer Press." Bell was also fired from the Storer faculty and lost his house the same year. He and Clifford continued to attack Brackett in the press.

After more than thirty years as the leader of Storer College, Nathan Brackett resigned to serve as treasurer. But the controversy was not over. Brackett defended himself in the *New York Age* in 1899. He wrote, "I am not in the habit of speaking in my own defense." He went on to attack J. R. Clifford's character, his newspaper, and his law practice, and wrote that all charges "are absolutely false in spirit and letter."

Finally, in May of 1900, a special investigating committee appointed by the Board of Trustees cleared Brackett of all charges. Teachers and clergy, many of them former students, defended Brackett too. They wrote and spoke with clarity, conviction, and reverence.

Nathan Brackett died ten years later on July 24, 1910, in Harpers Ferry. His defenders were echoed across many moving eulogies. No more love and admiration was ever offered in any other tributes to any other member of the Storer College family. Of all the words honoring Reverend Brackett, none reflected his character and summarized his service better than the speech of Rev. Henry M. Ford, a member of the Board of Trustees. At the dedication of a marble tablet to Brackett, Rev. Ford said, in part,

> Language is poverty-stricken in its ability to portray so rare a personality or in measuring so profound and useful a life…. He honored toil and gave it its rightful place. He taught us that work is not a curse, not something to shun, not something ignoble, but something dignified. I am not talking about the labor of the slave, but the labor of a free man who chooses it because he loves it and believes in it as a gift from Heaven.

CHAPTER 3

"There They Were—The Teachers!"

By Sarah White

In the months following the Civil War, the first batch of teachers began to arrive in Harpers Ferry, West Virginia, part of the hundreds of teachers that descended upon the Shenandoah Valley to educate more than 30,000 newly freed slaves. Their purpose: teach basic skills, such as reading, writing, and arithmetic, needed to survive in post-war, post-slavery America.

The young women were met with mixed emotions as they arrived. In a December 1866 dispatch to the New York *Independent*, journalist Mary Clemmer Ames wrote, "There they were—'The teachers!' The teachers! for whom Virginians had the most chivalric contempt, and the few Northern hearts here the warmest greeting." Ames relayed the "Virginia belle's" conviction that respectable women do not teach blacks, and that "every one who does…ought to be arrested and put into prison."

Local disdain for the teachers even went so far as barring the women from attending local churches. Not wanting to miss the Sabbath, the teachers were forced to hold services of their own. These meetings often took place in the Lockwood House, the home of Reverend Nathan Cook Brackett, who was the head of the Freewill Baptist

The Lockwood House was home and classroom to the early missionary teachers who came South to teach former slaves. The third floor was added in the late nineteenth century to house the rapidly expanding student population. Note the well pump in the yard. Indoor plumbing wasn't installed until the early twentieth century.

Home Mission Society primary school in Harpers Ferry. This home where they worshipped also had a classroom—the genesis of Storer College.

The Lockwood House, like other buildings in the area known as Camp Hill, was a survivor from the Civil War. One of the first teachers in Harpers Ferry recalled,

> …only a scene of desolation and ruin everywhere. Nearly all the public buildings and some dwelling-houses were partly torn down; trees and fences all burned; the debris of contending armies everywhere, and back of the house we are in, on Camp Hill, 300 soldiers' rude graves. The government houses we occupied were wrecked with shot and shell, but no hotel or boarding-house would admit us, so bitter was the feeling against persons who would teach colored people.

The damage inflicted included holes in the walls that allowed winds and other weather related elements to enter the interior. There were also reports of bats and other wildlife inhabiting the previously abandoned buildings. This, however, did not stop the newly arriving teachers from making the best of what they were given. The classrooms that had once been "defaced by war" were soon decorated with books and other classroom supplies.

The Freewill Baptists employed twenty-five teachers where the Shenandoah Valley crossed the borders of Virginia and West Virginia. Two of the early educators were

Sarah Jane Foster, one of the first four teachers to arrive in the Shenandoah from Maine to help educate newly freed slaves. (Photo courtesy of Wayne E. Reilly)

Sarah Jane Foster and Anne Dudley. The women had similar upbringings—both grew up in very religious, anti-slavery households in New England. As soon as they arrived in the Shenandoah Valley to teach, they faced public ridicule from the white communities. Both were soon able to find sanctuary with their African Americans students. While their early involvement with the school appeared to be homogenous, Anne and Sarah would each have very different experiences.

Sarah Jane Foster began her journey with the Freewill Baptist Home Mission Society in Martinsburg, West Virginia. When she started, she taught a class of nearly fifty students, a number that continued to grow. Twenty-six-year-old Sarah wrote daily in a diary and sent several letters detailing her experience to the Maine Baptist newspaper,

Zion's Advocate. In a letter dated December 16, 1865, she wrote that her students were "eager to learn, and some even come in several miles from the country, nights. One evening weekly is set apart for instruction in writing, which many need and earnestly desire…. Nearly all are doing well."

Sarah had a fairly close relationship with her students, especially one named John H. Brown, whom she wrote about frequently in her diary. In the same letter of December 16, 1865, she described, "One young man named John Brown, one of our outside committee, is really very intelligent…. He has proved an invaluable assistant in the school…. Color I find is no test of ability." Her devotion to educating in order to create equality—and being walked home in the evenings by her male students—displeased the whites in town. The situation became increasingly dangerous. She wrote on January 22, 1866:

Mr. Hoke seriously advised me to stay away from school tonight. He says that the roughs are terribly exasperated because I walked with Mr. Hopewell. Capt. McKenzie has volunteered to protect me to and from the school house and did so tonight. Mr. Hopewell and Mr. Brown stood guard by turns and we were not disturbed, though, coming around in the evening Capt. McKenzie saw indications that led him to go and get his pistol before coming around for me.

Five days later she despaired,

I am in trouble tonight. I have been slandered by the mob til Mrs. Hoke dare not board me. I can hardly blame her and yet it cuts me deeply. Mr. Brackett has come up to see about it. They say that I have walked night after night arm in arm with Colored men. It is a lie, and yet how can I prove it. God help me…. Oh Father let me stay. I cannot give up now.

Sarah continued to be heavily ridiculed for her dealings with the black community, and a rumored romance with Mr. Brown eventually led to her transfer from Martinsburg to Harpers Ferry. She arrived on Camp Hill on April 1, 1866. Her class sizes were much smaller than her previous school, and though she missed her Martinsburg students, she soon adjusted to Harpers Ferry, writing that the "wild scenery here suits and charms me." Unfortunately, she was only there about three months before the school year ended and she returned home to Maine.

Shortly after she arrived, Sarah received a devastating letter from the Home Mission Society. Her diary entry of July 23, 1866, begins, "As blue at heart as this ink tonight. I have just got a letter from Mr. Curtis to tell me that my commission will not be renewed this year. It is all because I had trouble in the Martinsburg school with the white outsiders. I can't blame myself." This, however, did not discourage her. A year following her dismissal, Sarah found a teaching position with the American Missionary Association. She began a school in South Carolina to teach the freedmen there

Anne Dudley Bates, an abolitionist before the Civil War, began teaching freedmen at war's end.

the necessary skills she had once taught in West Virginia. Regrettably, her time in South Carolina was short lived. Near the end of the school year in 1868, she contracted yellow fever, a disease that took the lives of many missionary teachers. Sarah died shortly after returning to Maine at the age of twenty-eight.

Another of Storer College's early teachers, Anne Dudley, had a much less tragic career at the school. Prior to teaching in the South, Anne worked actively against slavery as an abolitionist in Maine before the Civil War. She was called to education because she saw it as a duty to teach the freed slaves. Anne, just like Sarah Jane Foster, began her career as a teacher of the freedmen under the Freewill Baptist Home Mission Society. Her assignment was to begin a school in Charles Town, West Virginia. White residents of Charles Town adamantly opposed the idea. The local press and community severely criticized Anne for her work and even went as far as sending her death threats. On her first day of class, Anne had to be escorted by a "company of soldiers" due to "the promise of 'bloody head' and 'broken windows.'" This did not stop her though; she kept "a good axe and six-shooter at the head of my bed at night, resolved to sell my life as dearly as possible—if need be."

In an 1898 article for the *Missionary Helper*, the publication of the Free Baptist Woman's Missionary Society, Anne recalled that her first school "was in an old log house, with people living in the cellar, and a rough chamber over it where I lived the first term; and my next school room was an old log barn." In February 1866, she wrote to the *Freedmen's Mission*:

> No one can ever know the anxiety I have felt, and the effort I have had to make these two long months since I came here, occupying a rough log house, cold as a barn; teaching and boarding in the same room because I could not get board elsewhere…hearing a hundred different scholars recite lessons in a single day, doing my own work, receiving company, writing letters, etc., etc. All this and much more I have had to do in getting this school fairly started; and I can rejoice now in the belief that it will go on!

Anne continued to teach just as she was assigned to do and eventually found refuge with the African American population. After four months in Charles Town,

Young scholars earnestly study their lessons in Miss Cooke's classroom in Richmond, Virginia, just after the Civil War. The fancy clothing worn by the students and abundance of lesson books made a pleasing image, but Freedmen's schools were chronically short of funding and classroom materials. The teachers remained diligent and sincere in their efforts to educate African Americans.

Anne Dudley temporarily replaced Sarah Jane Foster in Martinsburg before moving to Harpers Ferry, where she remained for many years. "We stood alone, with little exception," she recalled, "and the struggle was intense for ten years."

In 1874, Anne left West Virginia to go to New York to marry Rev. L. E. Bates, but her involvement with the college did not end. Mrs. Bates continued to work with the Freewill Baptists—mainly women—to help raise money for the upkeep of the Storer College campus. She was even able to raise around $2,000 to help build a women's dormitory. In 1894, she returned to the campus to visit the new living quarters, writing in the *Missionary Helper:*

> Myrtle Hall! How I hoped, prayed, planned, and worked for it for years! Now my dream all came true and real! Myrtle Hall—house beautiful inside and out—was a delight to my eyes, in contrast to twenty-five years ago, when the girls were crowded in the old buildings, sometimes nine girls and three beds in a room, with all their work and study, with scanty food and fire, yet happy in having shelter, and kind teachers to help them.

Anne Dudley Bates continued to serve as a trustee for Storer College for the remainder of her life. She died July 28, 1923, at the age of ninety-one.

Coming to the South to educate the thousands of freed slaves following the Civil War required much more than teaching skills. The brave women who took on the job to teach were often met with criticism and threats from the local communities where they served. The experiences of Sarah Jane Foster and Anne Dudley Bates reveal that they had to possess the qualities of missionaries in a foreign land. Courage, determination, and survival skills set them apart from other teachers. The hard work and dedication of these young women helped start what Storer College stood for: work conquers all; and what America stands for: education and equality for all races, genders, and creeds in America.

CHAPTER 4

The First and Best Student

Adapted from GWWO, Inc./Architects
Edited by David Fox

I n an 1874 article for the *Baptist Union* newspaper about the beginnings of Storer College, one of the school's first teachers, Anne Dudley, wrote:

> Some of these students have a thrilling history from the cradle of slavery to the throne of freedom. One of them came into the school as tall as he is now, began with a primer, and accomplished the work of years in a single winter. With a perseverance that would stagger many young men, he has worked and studied, till he is now a most successful teacher and Christian worker, and is preparing for college with no thought but to press on.

Hamilton E. Keyes was already an adult when he appeared on the steps of the Lockwood House on Camp Hill in Harpers Ferry. Anne Dudley recalled the morning after she arrived in November 1865, "A load of straw stood at the door for beds. Mr. H. E. Keys [*sic*], who was one of our first pupils, said he could not sleep, when he knew

Storer College Glee Club, 1873. Hamilton Keyes is seated in the front row, second from the right.

the teachers had come, and had not beds so he came early with the straw."

Keyes hailed from Front Royal, Virginia, about fifty miles south of Harpers Ferry in the Shenandoah Valley. A check of the 1860 census for Virginia found no free blacks with the surname Keyes or Keys. Presumably then, Hamilton Keyes was born a slave and arrived in Harpers Ferry in 1865 with his freedom.

In April 1866, teacher Sarah Jane Foster first mentioned "Mr. Keyes (colored)" as a member of her party that visited Antietam Battlefield. On April 15, he joined the women teachers in "Mrs. Brackett's room and Mrs. B. read aloud...mostly from Tennyson." On May 2, 1866, Foster noted Keyes was teaching a Sabbath class, "a fine adult class who all read I believe."

Hamilton Keyes learned so fast in his first year that he traveled north with the missionaries at the close of school in June 1866 and was enrolled in the "Academical course" at Maine State Seminary in Lewiston, Maine, the following fall. There he shared room number 50 in Parker Hall with fellow Virginians John W. Dunjee (Dungy) and Alexander Sanders. Keyes and Dunjee continued at Maine State through the academic year 1867.

In July 1867, "Brother Hamilton Keyes" was hired to raise money among the "colored people" of the Shenandoah Valley toward the establishment of Storer College. He came back with $21, a considerable sum for the time, especially from an impoverished population. He was among the original incorporators of Storer College in September 1867. Keyes apparently enrolled in the Storer Normal School for its first year of operation. The 1868 Home Mission Society report noted that "three of our Normal pupils are now engaged in teaching." One was Keyes, who in January 1868 "opened a school [in Berryville, Virginia] which soon resulted in the formation of a church." In 1869, Hamilton Keyes served the Freewill Baptist Home Mission Society in Shepherdstown, West Virginia, but by the following year he and his wife were serving as missionaries in Cairo, Illinois.

Keyes returned to Storer College, at least during the years 1873-75, but was never listed among the graduates of any year. During these years at Storer he sang in the college glee club, the "Harpers Ferry Singers," and served as their advance agent as they performed in New England to raise money for the college. He eventually went to Hillsdale College and was ordained a Freewill Baptist minister. By 1889, Rev. Keyes was a member of the Storer College Board of Trustees.

CHAPTER 5

John Storer: A Northern Midnight Meeting and the Southern Mission Begins

By Dawne Raines Burke, PhD

In February 1867, Dr. Oren Burbank Cheney, then president of Bates College, traveled approximately sixty miles from his campus just outside Lewiston, Maine, to visit businessman John Storer in Sanford. This visit was certainly friendly, but it was also fraught with a purpose: to enlist Storer's financial assistance in support of education.

When Cheney arrived, he discovered that Storer was preparing to "execute a plan" that involved bequeathing $10,000 to an "organized body" having capacities to establish a school for freedmen—an institution that could evolve into a "permanent blessing to the colored race" in the South. Cheney asked, "Why not give the money to Free Baptists? They have always been true to the interests of the colored race? Some of their representatives are already at work establishing schools in the south."

After pondering, Storer announced to Cheney, "I should like to give it to your people, for I honor them for the position they have taken" against slavery.

After a long, introspective conversation that lasted until midnight, Storer had in effect committed $10,000 to the Free Baptists, provided the denomination organize a committee, raise matching funds, manage both the school and its endowment, and locate the school in a permanent facility with the potential for growth—all before January 1, 1868. To even the most casual observer, the task for the small denomination might have appeared overwhelming. Nonetheless, on February 6, 1867, Storer and Cheney wrote "out a plan for a Freedmen's College" in the South that was endorsed by both men.

John Storer was born on January 18, 1796, in the southeastern coastal town of Wells, Maine. When he was fourteen, he left his family to attend Bowdoin College, where he graduated in 1812. In 1820, at the age of twenty-four, Storer married Wells native Meribah Hobbs (with whom he

John Storer (1796-1867). The philanthropist's generous bequest made the founding of Storer College possible.

would have six children) and was working as a shipping clerk in Kennebunk for Benjamin Smith and Horace Porter when his employers suggested that lucrative business opportunities in shipping trades were possible for him in nearby Sanford. After being awarded statehood on March 15, 1820, Maine was primed for business, particularly along intercoastal waterways and rivers. If Storer was willing to relocate there, Smith and Porter would underwrite the business. Thus it was that Storer ended up in the river town of Sanford at a most opportune time, when the potential for capitalist ventures was rising and the question of slavery was gaining momentum.

In fact, New England as a whole was the center of anti-slavery sentiment, particularly among religious organizations. While conducting business between Sanford and Portland over the next four decades, Storer likely came in contact with several New England Baptists, Congregationalists, Unitarians, and Transcendentalists, many of whom were anti-slavery advocates organizing various aspects of their denominations' opposition to slavery. Reverend J. M. Brewster, pastor of a Free Baptist church two miles from Sanford, met Storer in the spring of 1863. Rev. Brewster wrote of Storer's connection to the faith:

> His wife, a Free Baptist, had died several years previous. His children had all married and settled in life. His housekeeper was a Free Baptist, and is now frequently seen at our denominational gatherings. Through her the light of the [*Morning*] *Star* shone in the household. Mr. Storer was not a member of any church, but was manifestly a sincere Christian.

Although Storer supported the Congregationalists, he frequented the company of Free Baptists during his lifetime because he "was deeply interested in the history and aims of [the] denomination." Storer witnessed the unswerving history of the small Free Baptist denomination as it began to unfold. His sentiments toward them are perhaps best described in one of the last letters he wrote before his death, dated October 3, 1867. In this missive directed toward the denomination, he claims, "'I knew your people more than sixty years ago, and have traced their progress with wonder and admiration since; and can but exclaim, 'What hath God wrought!'" This level of commitment to the denomination ultimately led Storer to proclaim to Cheney, during their 1867 wintry meeting, that because of "the position they [had] taken" against slavery he viewed the Free Baptists with "honor" for their strong sense of human dignity.

Unfortunately, before Storer could make the long journey to witness the fruits of his contributions first-hand, on October 23, 1867, at the age of 71, John Storer died after suffering an "attack of typhoid fever." According to historian Edwin Emery, Storer's death was precipitated by prolonged "grief at [Meribah's] death [seven years earlier] and anxiety on account of the war." Although Storer had been plagued throughout his life by periodic illnesses, Emery believed that the combination of these two events "completely broke him down and ended his life."

During his life, Storer—"a Whig and later Republican, though not an active partisan"—served the Sanford community as "selectman and member of the school com-

mittee," and for a year he acted as the postmaster of Springvale. Emery describes Storer as "a genuine contributor to charitable and religious organizations," adding that "during the Civil War no other man in town had the Union cause more at heart." After the war, Storer "offered to erect a monument in memory of the soldiers at Sanford." However, Sanford declined Storer's offer because of unspecified "conditions."

A large crowd attended Storer's burial service conducted on October 25, 1867. Two ordained Free Baptist ministers officiated the service. Several members of the congregation also attended, honoring the man as "fixed as the hills" when it came to two things: executing good business practices and supporting those less fortunate than he. Two weeks later, the *Morning Star* reported to the denomination body at large that John Storer "was not nominally a member of the Free Baptist denomination, but his sympathies had been more and more identifying him with us as a people," and that his "interest in the school which he really founded was very deep, and during the last weeks of his life he expressed great gratitude that God had permitted him to live to know that [Storer College] had become a fact."

It would now be up to the Free Baptists to make Storer's vision a reality.

CHAPTER 6

Faith and Work:
How Women and Prayer Laid the
Cornerstones of Storer College

By Autumn H. Cook

There is an old saying that "a woman's work is never done." The women of the
Free Baptist Woman's Missionary Society (FBWMS) were no exception to that
phrase. Their continuous philanthropic works toward Storer College exemplified the
notion. Though many never stepped foot on the ground of the school, and hardly any
of their names grace the text of our history books, these women were an integral part
of Storer. Cent by cent, prayer after prayer, and through the power of the written word,
they helped to build Storer College from afar.

Founded in 1873, the FBWMS voted a year later "that, so far as practicable, we
will endeavor to enlist our sisters in aiding the freedmen as well as the heathen, and
that it be left with the managers through what channel such aid shall be sent." By
1875, the women acted on that promise by sending the first missionary funded by their
society, Miss Lura Brackett, to Harpers Ferry. As the "lady principal" of the school,
Miss Brackett worked alongside her brother, Nathan Cook Brackett, the principal and
president of Storer College.

Every year from 1875 until at least 1921, the society gave to Storer College in
some way. Their range of contributions included: funding multiple missionary teachers and encouraging Free Baptist youth to fundraise; sending supplies for cooking
and sewing classes; and raising money to complete campus buildings. The breadth
of these women's works was likely more substantial considering there are many more
documents to discover concerning this subject, but what is already known certifies
that the Free Baptist Woman's Missionary Society made a very positive, meaningful,
and lasting impact on Storer College.

In 1878, Storer called upon the women to solve a problem. Myrtle Hall, the girls'
dormitory, was several years into construction but now suffered from lack of funds.
The building could not be completed without another thousand dollars. Lura Brackett
made a plea for assistance in the very first issue of the *Missionary Helper*, the society's
publication:

When a few years ago it was found that Storer College had outgrown its early
accommodations and ought to have a Girls' Hall, we thought the funds would
speedily be raised.... A few liberal donations in the beginning confirmed us
in this belief, and with promises of still more, we confidently laid the foundation....

Then there were months of waiting, with a growing demand to face, a
fainting hope to cherish, and the foundation ever before our eyes. How for-

Storer College teachers funded by the Free Baptist Woman's Missionary Society, 1899–1901, seated with President McDonald (back row) and Mr. Hughey: Stella James, Lura Brackett Lightner, Miss Johnston, Claire Sands, M. Jennie Baker, and Ella V. Smith.

lorn is the aspect of an unfinished and deserted building! – A ruin robbed of all sentiment, all picturesqueness! Last spring a friend suggested the idea of presenting our cause to the Sunday school scholars, and if possible to enlist their services in selling bricks, doors, windows, etc…. With a horror of debt, it is decided not to go on with work until enough has been contributed to enclose the building.

Two months later, Mr. Brackett wrote privately to the women, "We are almost discouraged. Six girls in a room, and more begging to come. But we will not run in debt, and we seem to be at the end of our resources. What shall we do?" Six ladies of the society gathered at the *Morning Star* office (home of the denomination's newspaper) in Dover, New Hampshire, to read the letter and pray for a solution. After the prayer, Mrs. Marilla Marks Hutchins Hills, a member of the board of managers of the society, proclaimed, "There is no time to get the consent of the Board, but it will consent. We will assume and raise that thousand dollars. Each of you write letters." Mrs. Hills also asked the editor of the *Morning Star*, "Will you stop the press while I write an appeal for a thousand dollars so we can go on with the girls' hall at Storer?"

Mrs. Hills' appeal appeared in both the *Morning Star* and the *Missionary Helper*. In part, it read:

A wailing, almost agonizing cry comes to us in behalf of our colored sisters in our Southern mission field....

More and more these freed young women crowded this fount of learning. The white inhabitants were not disposed to rent them rooms, and the necessity for increased accommodations became so pressing, that some five, perhaps more years ago, a movement was made to provide a Boarding Hall that would accommodate one hundred girls. The basement was finished and nearly enough brick burned to put up the walls, and then the building fund was exhausted. The committee in charge dared not incur a debt, and so the work was stayed. At length, words of encouragement and promise of further aid from that noble philanthropist and friend of the slave, Hon. Gerrit Smith, cheered the weary toilers at Harper's Ferry, and they rejoiced with great joy in the bright prospect of the speedy accomplishment of their enterprise. But alas! for human hopes. Almost immediately, like a clap of thunder in a clear sky, came the stunning intelligence that...Gerrit Smith had been suddenly summoned to his heavenly home.

Last year, another effort was made through the Sabbath schools and the Centennial Jubilee Singers, to raise $5,000, the sum required to finish the Hall. But this resulted in securing only about $1,500, and now the time has come to commence the work, in order to make the building available for use before another cold season. So there comes from the circumstances of the case, to the Free Baptist Woman's Mission Society, a piteous call for $1,000, a sum which added to the $1,500 on hand will put up the walls, and put on the roof. The building then, even in this unfinished state will shelter the girls and afford great relief....

Who will give $500? – $200? – $100? – $50? – $20? – $10? – $5? – $1? or even a smaller sum?

Money soon flowed forth to the treasurer of the society. Of the $1,774 sent to the treasurer between February and June, $1,068 was marked by donors to go toward the "Girls' Hall."

On May 30, 1878—the same week as graduation—the cornerstone of Myrtle Hall was laid. Mrs. Frances Stewart Mosher gave an address on behalf of the society, and over one thousand people gathered to watch as a sealed box of records was put into the stone and then the cornerstone cemented into place.

The fundraising for Myrtle Hall continued into the following year with the society's treasurer, Laura A. DeMeritte, asking for contributions toward doors, windows, and furnishings.

The building was formally dedicated on May 30, 1879, exactly one year after the cornerstone was laid. The president of the FBWMS, Mrs. Emeline S. Burlingame, spoke at this occasion:

Myrtle Hall, built in 1878, was used as a girls' dormitory with accommodations for sixty students and two faculty members. In 1914, it was completely renovated and modernized with the addition of central heat, electricity, and plumbing. Prior to that, rooms were heated by balky wood or coal furnaces, lighted with kerosene lamps, and bedrooms had chamber pots (slop jars) for nighttime bathroom needs.

When the call for help stirred our souls, a little over a year ago, it seemed almost impossible that a Society which, previous to that time, had in a whole year given but $350 to this school, could, in a comparatively short time, raise $1,000. But by trust in God, and by persevering and judicious effort, it was done and more than done....

This building has many owners. A little girl said a short time ago, "I want to go to Harper's Ferry some time and sleep in one of those rooms, for I own a brick in that building." In city, village, and country town, in the East and in the West, everywhere, are scattered those whose mites or larger sums are built into these walls and have given these doors and windows their places. The furnishings of these rooms have been planned and prepared by the busy brains and hands of women, very few of whom will ever see them in their destined places. May the young women who enjoy the privileges here afforded become imbued with the same desire to benefit others that has actuated these donors, and thus make this Hall the means of a great blessing to their race....

It is an inspiring thought that when we have all lain down to rest, this Hall will silently furnish successive generations of young women with opportunities for culture that they would not otherwise have enjoyed.

Contributing toward Myrtle Hall was the first time the society was asked to assist with completing a campus building at Storer, but it would not be the last. Just one year later in the July/August 1880 issue of the *Missionary Helper*, Mrs. Louise W. Brackett explained how the current chapel was not sufficient for graduation or for daily functions. She also mentioned that more teachers were needed at Storer. Her plea did not go unnoticed. Shortly thereafter, the monthly contributions listings at the end of each issue of the *Missionary Helper* showed donations notated with the phrase "Chapel Hall."

Also that summer, the Centennial Conference of the Free Baptists took place in Weirs, New Hampshire. There the foundation of Chapel Hall really began. In a private conversation Mr. Brackett said, "We have the boys and Lincoln Hall; we have the girls and Myrtle Hall, but no schoolroom. What can we do?" Since the schedule of the conference was set, there was no opportunity for a presentation regarding this need, but that did not stop the women. That same day, at noon, the Woman's Missionary Society decided to have a twenty-minute meeting. They prayed for a way to open a school building in Harpers Ferry. By the end of the day, word had spread and small pledges totaling two hundred dollars were in hand. But perhaps the true answer to their prayers came later that night, with the arrival of Mr. Lewis W. Anthony, a Rhode Island businessman, deacon, and new president of the Home Mission Society. Mrs. Frances Stewart Mosher gave an account of what transpired:

> That night on a late train Mr. Lewis W. Anthony and wife arrived from Providence, R. I. He told us afterwards that he could not sleep that night thinking of [his] five little children who rested in God's Acre. He woke his wife and… they decided to put a thousand dollars in memory of each child where it would

From the top: Mrs. Marilla Marks Hutchins Mills, Mrs. Emeline S. Burlingame, and Mr. Lewis W. Anthony, generous benefactors and supporters of the college.

help living young people. The next morning Mr. Anthony met a minister and asked, "Where would be a good place to invest a benevolent contribution?" The minister answered, "Well, the women are trying to raise money to put up a school building at Harper's Ferry." Half an hour later Mr. Brackett on the way to camp breakfast said, "Let me sit down. I am overcome with joy. Mr. Anthony offers $5000.00 for the school building if we will raise $5000.00 more." Mr. Anthony later told us of his night's experience and his belief that in some way he entered into the atmosphere of prayer.

Less than a year later, on May 30, 1881, the cornerstone was laid for the chapel hall, to be formally named Anthony Memorial Hall. On this occasion Frederick Douglass gave the oration. On the same date in 1882, the building was dedicated with Rev. Dr. Ransom Dunn of Hillsdale College giving the oration and Rev. Silas Curtis offering the prayer of dedication. May 30, 1883, would be the first time the building was used for graduation exercises, and on this occasion Mr. Lewis W. Anthony was asked to stand as everyone in attendance cheered for him.

The stories of these two buildings were just the beginning. The Woman's Missionary Society also played a part in the establishment of the Curtis Memorial Church, DeWolf Industrial Building, Lewis W. Anthony Industrial Building, Sinclair Cottage, President's Home, and the reengineering of the water supply to campus. Over the years the society also paid the salaries of numerous missionary teachers including Lura Brackett Lightner, Louise W. Brackett, Coralie Franklin, Kate C. Boothby, Marian G. Vale, Mary Brackett, Ella V. Smith, Marilla M. Brewster, M. Jennie Baker, Claire Sands, Stella James, Elizabeth Mosher McDonald, Mary E. Brady, Elizabeth L. Sims, Virginia Brown, Mary E. Peyton, Mabel Young, and Celeste Brackett Newcomer.

The work of the teachers, the work of those fundraising from afar, and the overall devotion of the FBWMS to Storer College did not go unnoticed by the students of the school. Letters of thanks were often documented in the *Missionary Helper*. In 1879, Etta Lovett wrote:

We, the Storer Normal girls, of Harper's Ferry, wish to express a word of thanks to our kind friends for their arduous work in befriending a struggling institution. We know somethings of the sacrifices that have been made by you. Though many, many miles separate us, it cannot lessen our esteem and gratitude towards you.

The men at the helm of the school also commended the women for their good works. Rev. Alexander Hatch Morrell said:

You will be thankful to know that the funds contributed have proved a very great blessing to the students, and yet you cannot understand how great unless you could be here and see the practical operation. I bless God to-day for the Woman's Missionary Society. If you never do any better than you have done for this branch of your excellent work it will pay for all your toil and endeavor. We did need the money you appropriated so much that I have looked upon it as a special interposition of Providence that you were inclined to bestow it.

Nathan Brackett offered his sentiments as well. "We wonder what would have been the fate of Harper's Ferry work but for the aid and inspiration given by the Woman's Missionary Society. Whatever of good has been accomplished at Storer College, a large share of it belongs to the credit of that organization."

Mr. Brackett's compliments inspire a thoughtful question: What would have been the fate of Storer College if not for the Free Baptist Woman's Missionary Society? Luckily, this question does not need an answer, because the women's beliefs and actions built roofs over heads, put teachers in classrooms, and gave educational opportunities to those who previously only dreamed of the possibility. And so, "Faith and works win," the motto of the society, stood true in the case of Storer College.

CHAPTER 7

"Where Doth Thy Rest, Alexander?"
The Mystery of the Final Resting Place of
Rev. Alexander H. Morrell

By James P. Madden

I n preparation for the 150th anniversary of the founding of Storer College, Harpers Ferry National Historical Park personnel, volunteers, and amateur sleuths increased their research efforts into the history of the school. Hundreds of hours have been spent studying the history of the school, but at least one significant mystery remains: the final resting place of Rev. Alexander Morrell, the spiritual leader during the school's formative years.

Rev. Morrell made his first trip to the Shenandoah Valley in the winter of 1864–65 while General Philip Sheridan's army was still lingering around Winchester. Closely involved with the formation of the Freewill Baptist Home Mission Society (FBHMS) and its mission to educate the recently freed slaves that were assembling in the Shenandoah Valley, Morrell had taken a sabbatical from his duties as minister of the church in Bath, Maine, to observe and serve. During this trip, he renewed his friendship with Rev. Nathan C. Brackett, who was serving as army chaplain and delegate of the United States Christian Commission assigned to General Sheridan. The two first became acquainted when Morrell served the Freewill

Rev. Alexander H. Morrell, spiritual leader of Storer College during its formative years.

Baptist church in Phillips, Maine, where he was instrumental in convincing Brackett to pursue a college education. Morrell later was a member of the council approving the ordination of Brackett as a minister.

The following year, the American Missionary Association, as well as the FBHMS, commissioned Brackett to serve as Superintendent of Free Schools in the lower Valley. The efforts of the Shenandoah Mission soon resulted in the West Virginia State Legislature issuing a charter for the formation of Storer College in 1867. The same year, at the age of forty-nine, Morrell answered the call from the Home Mission Board to return to Harpers Ferry as the spiritual leader of the college, allowing Brackett to devote his full time to his duties as principal of the school. In addition to serving the school,

Morrell was also charged with ministerial duties with the Free Schools throughout the Valley and establishing Freewill Baptist churches.

Arriving at Harpers Ferry with his wife and two young children, Morrell settled in the Lockwood House, "which was little but naked battered walls, only partially supplied with windows, and roof riddled by shells and cannon balls." They shared the nine-room house with the Brackett family, two lady teachers, several students, and meeting rooms. Morrell began his work among the poor and oppressed by visiting the surrounding towns and schools in West Virginia, across the Potomac River in Maryland, and up the Shenandoah Valley. He came to know all the students at Storer and led them in revivals that sometimes lasted for weeks, gathering every night and often early in the morning.

His dear friend and colleague, Nathan Brackett, wrote,

> Sometimes when presenting the infinite love of God to the crowds of Freedmen that came to listen, his conception of the plan of salvation through Jesus Christ became so vivid, his longing to save men so intense, that we saw his tear-stained face shining, "as it had been the face of an angel." Though he never sought to arouse the noisy demonstrations which were characteristic of the worship of those days, but rather to substitute for them, reflection, high resolves and honest purposes, yet every now and then the storm would come with such tremendous violence, the air ringing with such wild hallelujahs, as nearly to take away the senses of one not accustomed to it. At such times, with wide open windows and doors, we had the prostrate forms of the shouters carried out of doors, and sang a long metre hymn till order was restored and then went on with the meeting.

Morrell also succeeded in forming several churches in West Virginia as well as "old Virginia." This schedule of constant travelling, preaching, and organizing eventually proved too much for him, and at the end of the school term he was forced to return to his home in Maine to regain his health.

In 1870, however, Rev. Morrell returned to his duties at Harpers Ferry and settled his family into what would henceforth be known as the Morrell House. The house contained eleven rooms but once again was shared with as many as twenty-seven students until the completion of Myrtle Hall in 1879. Morrell resumed his activities, preaching and counseling with the same fervor as before, meeting all students upon their arrival and guiding them through their period of adjustment. Working side by side, Morrell and Brackett shared the same passion of providing educational opportunities for the freed people and laid the foundation for the school that produced hundreds of African American educators.

Once again in 1881, poor health forced Morrell to step back from his rigorous duties and accept the position of pastor at the Freewill Baptist church in Chepachet, Rhode Island. In 1885, he resigned this post and announced his intention to return to Harpers Ferry and resume his duties at the college. In December, he reached the

The Morrell House, one of the first four government houses used in the early days of Storer College. Like the others, it had suffered from wartime damage and neglect. Rev. Morrell and his family shared the house with Storer students. This photo shows a restored building now used as headquarters for Harpers Ferry National Historical Park.

home of his son in Irvington, New Jersey, where he again fell ill. He remained there until his death at ten p.m. on Friday, December 24, 1885.

Morrell's life is well documented in the archives of the *Free Baptist Cyclopaedia*, the Freewill Baptist newspaper the *Morning Star*, and the college itself, where the Board of Trustees soon passed a resolution honoring Morrell:

> Whereas it has pleased Almighty God to remove from our midst after a brief and painful illness our deceased brother and fellow laborer Reverend Alexander Hatch Morrell, and this creates a vacancy in the body that we cannot hope to fill, therefore, be it <u>Resolved</u> that we the Board of Trustees of Storer College, do hereby record our greatest sorrow at his death and our high appreciation of his long and faithful services as a member of the Board and a friend of this institution.

But the mystery remains as to the location of his final resting place. In a testimonial often referred to as Morrell's obituary, Rev. Brackett states:

> There was no question where we should bury him, for all knew for whom and what his life was given, and that he wished his body to rest at Harper's

Ferry. The whole community, regardless of color, came out to testify their respect at the burial, which took place Sunday, Dec 27, just two weeks after he preached his last sermon. The tributes from white and colored at the funeral were hearty and generous.

Here the mystery unfolds—there is neither a headstone in the Harper Cemetery or any reference to a Morrell burial in the records of Jefferson County or the cemetery.

Over the years, experts and amateurs alike have been unable to explain why their research fails to discover any confirmation of the funeral in area newspapers or any oral history from a family member. Morrell had obviously earned the respect of both the black and white communities of Harpers Ferry and had long been a prominent and highly visible citizen whose sudden passing would not go unnoticed.

The presumed final resting place for Alexander Morrell in the churchyard of Curtis Freewill Baptist Church. (National Park Service, photo by Autumn Cook)

On February 23, 1886, the board drafted a resolution for a memorial of some kind to honor Reverend Morrell: "Resolved further, that it is the sense of this meeting that some fitting memorial of his high Christian character and his invaluable services be erected in around the college buildings, as an expression of the gratitude and love of his many friends who now mourn his loss."

A monument in memory of Morrell stands today on the grounds of the Curtis Freewill Baptist Church on the former campus of Storer College, near the corner of Jackson and Fillmore streets. According to a 2010 National Park Service Cultural Landscape Inventory report, the monument was "placed on the Storer College property along Jackson Street" and "remains on its original site." However, according to a Historic American Building Survey report on the church, the monument was originally erected in "front of the Lockwood" House and later moved to the present location. The highly credible source for the Lockwood reference was a June 1887 issue of the *Pioneer Press*, a Martinsburg newspaper published by John R. Clifford, a Storer College graduate in 1875 and the first African American lawyer admitted to the bar in West Virginia. A confirmation of the monument being moved to its present location was recently discovered in an article in the Free Baptist Women's *Missionary Helper* publication, describing the rededication of the monument in the churchyard in 1899, but no mention of disinterment of Morrell's remains.

Why would the monument be placed in front of the Lockwood House instead of the Morrell House? The Lockwood House is adjacent to the cemetery, and the author's suggestion is that the monument was placed on the Morrell gravesite, which was located either in the Harper Cemetery, "in front of the Lockwood" House, or in the lawn of the Lockwood House, next to the cemetery. The funeral service occurred on a Sunday, less than forty-eight hours following Morrell's death, and possibly there was no time for burial arrangements in the cemetery, causing the burial to be on school property, hence no cemetery record of the burial.

At the 1951 Storer College Founder's Day celebration, former President Henry T. McDonald paid tribute to Morrell, "whose body lies under the monument in Curtis Memorial church-yard," but no proof of this fact is cited. If it is accepted that the monument was erected on the gravesite and later moved to its present location, it is probable that Morrell's remains were moved at the same time to the new monument location. Historical purists are still bothered by the fact that no documented proof is found to confirm a disinterment. Based upon documentation at hand, it appears that Morrell rests either under the monument or in an unmarked grave located either in the cemetery or on the college grounds "in front of the Lockwood" House. There has been recent discussion about the utilization of Ground Penetrating Radar in an effort to resolve this lingering mystery, but at least until that time, the question remains:

"Where Doth Thy Rest, Alexander?"

Editor's note: Under the supervision of park staff, the site surrounding the Morrell monument adjacent the Curtis FWB Church was investigated with Ground Penetrating Radar (GPR) the last week of April 2017. The GPR data suggest strongly that there is a feature beneath the ground on the east side of the monument. The depth, size and orientation of this feature indicate a possible burial site. Based upon the information derived from the research surrounding the "Morrell Mystery" and the alternative suggestion that a man of such stature would not be forgotten, most experts have agreed that the concern over Morrell's final resting place may itself be laid to rest.

CHAPTER 8

The Measure of a Man

By Connie Park Rice, PhD

"When a boy I was a farmer, then a waiter, next a barber, then a teacher, next an editor and last a lawyer and the first to be admitted to practice in my state. I used them all as a means to the final end."

—J. R. Clifford

John Robert Clifford (1848-1933) was many things: bold, outspoken, stubborn or determined (depending on the point of view), principled, intelligent, and often, arrogant. Some men called him fearless, brilliant, and a "devoted race man." Other men, in an attempt to denigrate him, labeled him an "infidel" or referred to him as "Cuffy." A civil rights pioneer, Clifford challenged the segregated legal status of African Americans in West Virginia courtrooms in the decades before and after 1900, an era marked with growing discrimination, disenfranchisement, and segregation against black Americans. Born into the free black family of Isaac and Mary Clifford amid the western mountains of the slave state of Virginia, Clifford rose to prominence through hard work and perseverance.

From a young boy who could not read or write and made his "mark" to enlist in the Civil War, Clifford's desire for knowledge led him to become a member of civil rights activist W. E. B. Du Bois's "talented tenth," a founding member of the Niagara Movement, and a member in the American Negro Academy, the first major intellectual society for African Americans in the United States. First a farmer, then a soldier, barber, laborer, teacher, editor, and finally an attorney, he continually strove to improve not only himself, but the social, economic, and political status of all African Americans.

J. R. Clifford

Frequently, his quest for equal rights ignited racial, class, and political conflict that resulted in attacks against his newspaper, Martinsburg's *Pioneer Press*, as well as physical attacks against his person.

Much of Clifford's success can be attributed to the education, morals, and principles he obtained at Storer College in Harpers Ferry, West Virginia. Believing that man's "true dignity begins in the mind" and is "the source of all that is great in him," Clifford moved to Harpers Ferry to attend Storer College in the fall of 1873. Admission to the school required students to "give satisfactory evidence of good moral char-

Founding members of the Niagara Movement: W. E. B. Du Bois (seated) and (left to right) J. R. Clifford, L. M. Hershaw, and F. H. M. Murray. Clifford helped secure the campus of Storer College for the Movement's second annual meeting in 1906.

acter," and offered an education to those of any race and gender who were "ladies and gentlemen." In a place imbued with John Brown's legacy of courage, conviction, and hope for full equality, Clifford saw hope in a college that promised to lift African Americans both morally and intellectually. Brown's legacy and the self-discipline and moral values instilled in the students of Storer College became a part of Clifford's life. The ethical principles that he learned and practiced—hard work, perseverance, and the concepts of duty and obligation—he used as tools in his struggle for civil rights.

While Clifford was a student at Storer, at midnight on August 13, 1874, a crowd gathered at the county jail in nearby Martinsburg, West Virginia. They took John Taliaferro, a black man accused of attempted rape and murder, and lynched him. Regardless of his innocence or guilt, Taliaferro's lynching accentuated for Clifford the need for African Americans to obtain full civil and political rights, and convinced him that, "people who do not contend for their rights cannot expect to get them, or if gotten, cannot expect to retain them," and that cowardice "induces silly fellows to do you harm" and makes men "subject to so many injustices." From that day forward, Clifford boldly asserted his rights, for himself and for his race without "remorse or conscience," a stance that often placed him in conflict with Republican Party leaders and, eventually, the administrators at Storer College.

After graduating from the Storer College Normal School in the spring of 1875, Clifford became the first black principal of the Sumner School in Martinsburg. In December 1876, Reverend Nathan Brackett, President of Storer College, officiated the marriage of Clifford and his fellow Storer graduate, Mary E. Franklin, at a ceremony in Harpers Ferry.

Throughout the 1870s, Clifford became more politically active, spending his "time and means" campaigning throughout the state for Republican candidates. At the time, the Republican Party was comprised mainly of Northern white Protestants, businessmen, farmers, factory workers, and African Americans, while the Democratic Party was primarily whites in the former slave-holding South. Clifford frequently campaigned for William H. H. Flick, a childhood friend and author of the Flick Amendment, when he was the Republican candidate for the West Virginia Supreme Court of Appeals in 1876 (and, again, in 1880, when Flick ran for the United States Congress). Clifford also at-

Mary Clifford, 1907 graduate of Storer College and daughter of J. R. and Mary Franklin Clifford.

tended the first African American convention in the state led by Robert W. Simmons of Parkersburg in 1876.

When Reverend J. W. Dunjee of Winchester, Virginia, came to speak in Martinsburg that year, Clifford claimed he was the first "Negro" Democrat he had ever seen. Clifford offered to find him a place to speak and to protect him knowing that local blacks, who were fiercely Republican, would be hostile to Dunjee. Armed with stones and clubs, Clifford and a few friends defied over fifty African Americans who threatened to attack Dunjee. After the incident, Clifford argued that all men should be allowed to speak and offered to debate Dunjee publicly if the black community would give him a proper hearing. Unfortunately, numerous members of the black community saw Clifford's defense of Dunjee as disloyalty to the Republican Party and, therefore, traitorous to the black community. Nathan Brackett called Mr. Dunjee "the worst man living" who had done the Baptist "denomination an irreparable wrong" by supporting Democratic candidate Samuel Tilden in his bid for the presidency. Yet years later, after Dunjee returned to the Republican fold, Brackett not only welcomed him back into the Baptist Church, he made him the pastor of Storer College's chapel.

Between 1876 and 1884, Clifford became increasingly critical of the local party leadership and their failure to adhere to the original principles of the party. His establishment of the *Pioneer Press* in 1882 provided him with a public platform for his outspoken defense of civil rights and his continued criticism of the Republican faction in charge. The conflict escalated in 1884 when this sect appointed one of their own as Postmaster—a man who participated in the Taliaferro lynching—and ousted another Republican, J. Nelson Wisner, a lawyer and owner of the *Martinsburg Independent* where Clifford's newspaper was published. The *Press* led a petition of 132 black voters in opposing the appointment. As a result, the leading Republicans schemed to have Clifford arrested on trumped up charges of larceny, bribery, and forgery. He was found "not guilty" on all charges. Clifford's support of Wisner in the factional fight also led him in direct conflict with William H. H. Flick. In May, when the State Republican Convention voted to elect Clifford as a delegate to the national convention, Flick went from delegate to delegate and had each change his vote. That year Clifford declared himself independent in politics and stated that he believed in voting for "men and not parties" (later becoming "for men and measures, not parties").

Wisner allowed Clifford to read law with him, and when Wisner ran for Congress as an Independent in 1886, Clifford supported him over Republican William H. H. Flick. Nathan Brackett immediately criticized Clifford for his stance. Clifford discussed his decision with his former principal, yet Brackett wrote a newspaper editorial claiming, "There is no use in denying the fact, colored men have no faith in a colored Democrat. To every man, and doubly so to the women he is a traitor to his race." For Clifford, racial interests superseded party loyalty. Brackett had worked with Democrats to defeat Republicans in the past, and willingly accepted Rev. Dunjee after his being a "colored Democrat." Clifford wrote during these times, "[We] thought it impossible to be independent in politics, but 'wise men change, fools never!… We do not ask the colored men of this State to be democrats—but we do ask them to be *independent men*—a thing impossible by cursing all other parties and sticking to a party that curses you."

By the 1890s, the desire for national unity and the rise of Jim Crow segregation across the South increased the pressure on black colleges and their administrators, including Brackett and the Storer College Board of Trustees, to train students for service and industrial trades in addition to academic or professional fields. A few years earlier, Storer students and their parents had begun to urge Brackett to add more industrial classes. Former student and teacher Coralie Franklin wrote that "a skillful hand, as well as a cultivated brain is the crying need of the hour." Clifford himself expounded on the necessity of students obtaining the skills and working hard until they obtained the position they wanted. While cautious of the shift toward education in the trades, Storer alumni were optimistic that the school would remain true to its intellectual mission.

Racial conflicts escalated in 1896 after the Board of Trustees instructed Brackett to close a building on campus that had been used for boarding African American visitors to Harpers Ferry in the summer months. Other buildings on campus, although leased by African Americans, continued to board white visitors. A protest meeting led by "Alumni and friends" erupted over the decision. For African Americans, Harpers Ferry was a place to connect to their history and their fight for freedom, a place open to African Americans when access to so many places was denied. Storer College, sitting on hallowed ground, with a mission of education for all, enhanced that sense of belonging. Successful elite and middle-class African American visitors provided examples to Storer students of what they could achieve with hard work and education; and black businesses in the region benefitted from the money they spent. Clifford and other alumni saw the decision as an abandonment of the college's original mission, a failure to maintain its principles, and a capitulation to Jim Crow.

Condemning the decision, "Alumni and friends" drafted several resolutions against Brackett's administration but none were passed. Clifford, however, continued the fight against Brackett in the *Press* and in the court, filing a formal lawsuit against the college principal over a real estate disagreement and calling for Brackett's resignation. Brackett and his supporters charged Clifford with inflaming racial tensions and accused him of being a self-seeking failure. Clifford's allegations of moral violations, improperly ordaining ministers, and poor business practices against Brackett that appeared in the *Pioneer Press* may have contributed to a decline in enrollment. Under emotional pressure and in poor health, Brackett resigned as principal in 1898 after leading the school for thirty-three years. In 1899, he asked Storer's Board of Trustees to investigate all charges, and six months later the board vindicated Brackett. The quarrel led to years of bitterness and public allegations. Six decades later, Brackett's daughter Mary criticized Clifford's *Pioneer Press* as "a very nasty, hostile, and unprincipled sheet," that was "a thorn in the flesh for Storer for many years." Still, Clifford continued to maintain ties with Storer College. He made arrangements for the 1906 meeting of the Niagara Movement held at Storer, and his daughter Mary graduated from Storer in 1907.

Principles and character guided the life of John Robert Clifford. They were essential to his concept of manhood, his social values, his spiritual beliefs, and his political ideology. Despite his criticism of the Republican Party, he remained, at heart, a Republican. His disillusionment with the Republican Party stemmed from anger, an emotion he shared with millions of other black Americans, at the party's failure to adhere to what he believed was its original principles. More importantly, he wanted the American people to have honor and patriotism enough to live up to the principles established in the Declaration of Independence and the American Constitution. Throughout his lifetime, Clifford expected and demanded all of the rights and privileges of an American citizen and, as a civil rights pioneer, he refused to settle for anything less.

CHAPTER 9

A Beloved Daughter of Storer: Coralie Franklin Cook

By Connie Park Rice, PhD

A true "child" of Storer College, Coralie Franklin Cook, educator, suffragist, and civil rights activist, was part of the first generation of children to come out of bondage and step into the academic world. Born in Lexington, Virginia, Coralie Franklin was emancipated at age four and began her education after the Civil War in a Winchester, Virginia, school "conducted by two brave, earnest, Christian ladies from Maine." It was there as a small girl that Miss Franklin first met Reverend Alexander H. Morrell, the spiritual leader of Storer College, who also had ministerial duties in Free Schools throughout the Shenandoah Valley. She distinctly remembered the "kind gentleman with the pleasant voice and tender eyes, who placed me on his knee, saying to my mother, 'Well, this little one will not be a slave.'"

Coralie Franklin Cook

Several years later Coralie moved to Harpers Ferry with her parents, Albert and Mary C. Franklin, and her sister, Mary Elizabeth, to greet "Mr. Morrell as pastor, and find in him a family friend." Miss Franklin attended Storer's Preparatory School and graduated from Storer Normal School. Around age seventeen, she began teaching in the small village of Knoxville, Maryland, just a few miles east of Harpers Ferry. Her small log schoolhouse sat adjacent to the C&O Canal, with a "gurgling, clear little brook running by its side." In 1878, she wrote a letter to a Free Baptist Sunday school class in Portland, Maine, about her school:

> Did you ever visit a colored school before? It is Friday afternoon, the lessons have all been said, and as the bell is tapped every book is laid aside. The arms are folded, and many pairs of bright eyes are directed toward my table. Then I read a story and talk about it until they thoroughly understand it…. I then remind the children of the Sabbath school, and when some of them grieve because their clothes are not better, I tell them to come clean and whole, and God will not mind the coarse patched dress or coat if the heart is right. Then with a polite bow and smiling faces they all file out on their way home.

Miss Franklin went on to graduate from Storer's Academic Department in 1880. She then studied elocution at Boston's Emerson College, Martha's Vineyard Summer Institute of Oratory, and was one of three black students accepted into the Shoemaker School of Oratory in Philadelphia, Pennsylvania. In 1881, she returned to West Virginia to become the first African American female instructor at Storer, teaching elocution, or the art of public speaking and reading.

The Free Baptist Woman's Missionary Society funded Miss Franklin's $200 annual starting salary. She often wrote of her experiences in Harpers Ferry for the Society's publication, the *Missionary Helper*. In October 1882, she provided a summary of the previous school year for their annual report, though prefaced it by writing that "to give a report of its labors that would convey any adequate idea of the hopes and fears, the joys and sorrows, the benefits and blessings that fell to the lot of teachers and pupils at Storer, would require a skillful pen." She described with some sadness the difference between her young and older pupils:

> [It] is much harder to learn one's letters at thirty than at six; harder to understand long division at forty than at eight; and harder still to put one's pride in the pocket, and go day after day into classes with those so much younger. It is at such times as these that the unbidden tears rush to your eyes, as you guide the untutored hand in forming letters, and think, "O, how willingly would I learn for you, if I could." But they do learn. I cannot tell you how many came to us last fall unable to write their names, who, when they left in the spring, could write a letter. There is one thing of which I am certain. The problem of negro education has been solved, and Storer Normal School is helping with the demonstration.

In addition to her teaching experiences, Miss Franklin's correspondences to the *Missionary Helper* detailed temperance meetings, Sunday school classes, commencement exercises, and the progress of literacy in the South. In March 1885, she wrote, "It is no small pleasure to note the wonderful improvement in everyday life that Christianity and education are making among the people." She understood the struggles her students faced to be in a classroom and the importance of her work. "The need of schools like ours is greater, if possible, than ever before. It belongs, to the graduates of these institutions to go forth waging war against the great mass of illiteracy at the South which threatens to be an evil second only to that of slavery itself."

In Harpers Ferry, Miss Franklin built a reputation as a talented speaker. Her brother-in-law and owner of the *Pioneer Press* in nearby Martinsburg, John R. Clifford, wrote of her elocution skills, "to be master of this inestimable blessing gives tribble force to every other accomplishment; happiness to the sick chamber, satisfaction to the social circle, and glory to the soul." As early as 1877, John Wesley Cromwell, editor of the *People's Advocate* in Washington, DC, described Miss Franklin as "an elocutionist of grace, skill and power."

In January of 1887, Miss Franklin became the editor of the "Women's Column"

Early students and faculty of Storer College including Rev. Nathan Brackett and his wife Louise (center of photo) and Coralie Franklin (standing on right in striped dress). Like many African Americans in this photo, Miss Franklin was a descendant of slaves. Her ancestor Elizabeth Hemings was a slave at Thomas Jefferson's Monticello.

published in the *Pioneer Press*. The column included original writings from Coralie Franklin and other women across West Virginia, as well as articles on women's issues from other newspapers. She also became a founder and president of the Mount Hope Woman's Christian Temperance Union at Harpers Ferry—the first African American branch of the organization in West Virginia.

Between 1891 and 1893, Miss Franklin divided her time between teaching at Storer College and teaching English and elocution at Howard University in Washington, D. C. Her work in Washington offered her access to events and people engaged in topics close to heart: education, suffrage, and civil rights. There she continued to gain prominence on the state and national level.

In 1892, Miss Franklin spoke at the West Virginia Teachers Association, an organization founded for African American teachers (1891-1954). That same year she joined Washingtonians Anna Julia Cooper and Mary Church Terrell to form the Colored Women's League for the promotion of African American women's concerns. Named superintendent of the National Home for Destitute Colored Women and Children in Washington, DC, she resigned her position at Storer College in 1893 and relocated permanently to the District of Columbia. In letters to the *Storer Record*, the college newspaper, Coralie Franklin's continued devotion and love for her alma mater was clear. In February 1894, she wrote, "I am busy and happy in my new field of labor. In spirit I mingle with teachers and pupils of you each day. Whatever of discouragement or distress may come to you, I share with you and whatever of success or encouragement is yours is mine also." Later that year, she became one of the first women appointed as a trustee to the college.

Coralie Franklin Cook spent her life advocating for the rights of women, African Americans, and the disadvantaged.

In an address at the League of Women's 1895 conference in Atlanta, Georgia, Miss Franklin discussed the opportunities for self-advancement and education available to African American women and how the National League of Colored Women aided aspiring women who were hampered and held back from the attainment of their ambitions. Her address came on the heels of Booker T. Washington's famous "Atlanta Compromise" address delivered on September 18, 1895, that claimed the "Negro problem" would be solved by a policy of gradualism and accommodation.

Miss Franklin disagreed with Washington's policy of accommodation, particularly in 1896 when Storer College appeared to block African American boarders while continuing to accept white boarders. That summer, she led the DC Colored Women's League on a pilgrimage to John Brown's Fort, then located on the Murphy Farm in Harpers Ferry. The women resolved that the action taken by Storer College administrators merited their "severest censure and disapproval," for their willingness to "sacrifice manhood rights to mercenary motives" leading to "an example of treachery and prejudice from a hitherto trusted quarter."

Later that year, Miss Franklin was part of a joint committee of fourteen women selected to create a plan for a merger of the National League of Colored Women and the National Federation of African American Women, where she played a vital role in the creation of the National Association of Colored Women (NACW). Despite her concerns over the management of Storer, Miss Franklin's love of her alma mater and her commitment to its educational mission continued. She wrote to the *Storer Record* in 1897: "There's a heart to heart life there that I at least, have never found anywhere else."

In 1898, Miss Franklin married George W. Cook, a Howard University professor and trustee. She continued to be an outspoken advocate for education, women's rights, social uplift, and racial equality. In August of 1899, she attended the second NACW Convention in Chicago, Illinois, and in February of 1900, she delivered an address to honor Susan B. Anthony at her eightieth birthday celebration and retirement from the National American Woman's Suffrage Association (NAWSA) held at the Lafayette Opera House in Washington, DC titled "Greetings from the Colored Women," Coralie

In the summer of 1896, Coralie Franklin led the DC Colored Women's League on a pilgrimage to John Brown's Fort. A decade later, members of the Niagara Movement, predecessor to the NAACP, would make the same pilgrimage during their meeting in Harpers Ferry.

Franklin Cook praised Anthony for realizing "the all-important truth that no woman and no class of women can be degraded and all womankind not suffer thereby" and thanked her on "behalf of the hundreds of colored women who wait and hope with you for the day when the ballot shall be in the hands of every intelligent woman; and also in behalf of the thousands who sit in darkness and whose condition we shall expect those ballots to better, whether they be in the hands of white women or black…" Yet despite her kind words for Anthony, African American women who attended the event were "compelled to walk" the stairs as the elevator "was reserved for whites."

At the age of forty, in December of 1901, Coralie Franklin Cook gave birth to her only child, George W. Cook, Jr. Her work to improve education and achieve social justice continued on the national and international stage. In 1913, disillusioned with the entrenchment of Jim Crow and the failure of the NAWSA to include black women on an equal basis, Coralie and her husband George became members of the Baha'i Faith. Convinced the Baha'i principles of the unity of mankind, peace without animosity or prejudice, and equality between men and women would bring positive change to the African American community, she organized Baha'i meetings for Howard University students. Claiming, "I must live my life where I am placed," she believed her faith could open racial attitudes. In a March 1914 letter to 'Abdu'l-Baha, the Baha'i leader, Coralie described the historical consequences of racial prejudice, stating, "Weary and heart sore, discouraged with the Churches that close their doors to them, the silent pulpits that should thunder forth in trumpet tones against the iniquities in the pews, it were strange indeed if the Baha'i teachings wakened no response of great hope in the hearts of colored people."

Coralie Franklin Cook served on the DC Board of Education from 1914 to 1926, a time of increased racial tension and race riots across the nation. She belonged to the Free Baptist Woman's Missionary Society, the Board of Public Welfare, the Juvenile Protection Association, the Red Cross, and was an early member of the National Association for the Advancement of Colored People (NAACP).

Coralie Franklin Cook always envisioned a better world, with opportunities and equality for all. Yet while she worked "where she was placed," she encouraged her son to study and work abroad—and he did so from 1930 to 1944. When she died in 1942, her son and heir was interned in a German prison camp in occupied France. In addition to her final bequest to him, she provided an endowment for Storer College, a final "gift from a beloved daughter."

CHAPTER 10

The Promise of Storer College

By John Lustrea

Of all the speeches that Frederick Douglass gave in his long life, the one at Storer College on May 30, 1881, must have felt different. The occasion was Decoration Day, the precursor to modern-day Memorial Day, and the date Storer had chosen as its Anniversary Day. The college had also selected that day to lay the cornerstone for the planned addition to Anthony Hall. It wasn't Douglass' most famous speech, but it was considered one of the greatest speeches ever given at Storer. He reflected on John Brown's 1859 raid on Harpers Ferry, an excursion in which Brown had earnestly asked Douglass to participate, even offering to defend him with his life. Douglass had countered his friend's offer by saying that Harpers Ferry was "a perfect steel trap; once in you will never get out alive." Douglass had been right, and we can only wonder what was playing through his mind the day of the speech and how it must have felt to be so close to the place where Brown had made his final stand.

Over the course of thirty-six hours in October 1859, while capturing the United States Armory and Arsenal at Harpers Ferry in an attempt to seize weapons and start

U.S. Marines storm the engine house in this Frank Leslie's Illustrated Newspaper *depiction of John Brown's Raid. Brown was captured, tried, and executed for his crimes. His actions to end slavery led many Northern abolitionists, including Frederick Douglass, to view Brown as a martyr.*

a slave revolt, Brown and what he referred to as his "Provisional Army" had been surrounded by townspeople, militia, and U.S. Marines. Ten of his twenty-one men had been killed; six had been captured, tried and executed; the remainder had escaped. Brown's actions had produced a firestorm of controversy. The violent attempt by a white man from the North to free slaves in the South concerned countless Southerners and embittered them to the North. Scholars have debated Brown's specific goal and how much violence he had planned for the Harpers Ferry raid. We can be sure that Brown's ultimate objective was to free as many slaves as possible through any means necessary, an almost unheard-of stance for a white man to take in 1859. Douglass' first meeting with Brown had confirmed this. When he had first dined at the Brown residence in 1848, he had been encouraged to sit at the table while Brown's family waited on him—at the time, a radical act for a white family. Laudable though Brown's racial attitudes may have been, the issue for many, both now and then, was Brown's willingness to resort to violence in his crusade against slavery. Even Abraham Lincoln echoed this sentiment, saying, "Though he agreed with us in thinking slavery wrong. That cannot excuse violence, bloodshed, and treason."

In 1881, Douglass offered a revised portrait of John Brown to his audience. Up until then Brown had been considered a crazed fanatic who thrilled in violently freeing slaves and whose ultimate goal was a massive slave rebellion throughout the South. Douglass depicted him as a martyr instead. This was not a new position. Henry David Thoreau and other Northerners had called John Brown "an angel of light" just days after the raid. But Douglass was the first to present so sympathetic a portrait of John Brown in such a public manner in the town where Brown was captured.

Not only was Brown a martyr, Douglass argued, but he was ahead of his time. "More than twenty years have rolled between us and the Harper's Ferry raid, though since then the armies of the nation have found it necessary to do on a large scale what John Brown attempted to do on a small one." Douglass here was referring to the fratricidal conflict between the North and South. Within eighteen months of the Harpers Ferry raid, the Civil War had erupted. In 1863, (more than three years after Brown's actions) the Emancipation Proclamation had made it the policy of the Union army to set Southern slaves free, by force if necessary. Two years later, Northern victory had resulted in the passage of the Thirteenth Amendment to the Constitution, which legally ended slav-

John Brown.

Frederick Douglass (1818 -1895)

ery. Thus, the cause for which Brown had been executed six years earlier became the law of the land.

The agitation of Frederick Douglass was a significant factor in the progress of American race relations, but the famous orator placed Brown above himself in the pantheon of abolitionists. "I could live for the slave, but [Brown] could die for him." Douglass would go on to say that Brown was like "the great and good of all ages—the men born in advance of their times, the men whose bleeding footprints attest the immense cost of reform, and show us the long and dreary spaces, between the luminous points in the progress of mankind." According to Douglass, this was the true value of John Brown. Douglass' address was published and the sales were put toward a John Brown professorship at Storer to educate future students through the lens of Brown's virtues.

The newspaper coverage of the event was minimal. The only reason there was much coverage at all was due to Douglass' involvement. The accounts of the event shared many similarities. They all mentioned the presence of several Confederate veterans in the audience, though their reactions were not recorded. The lack of explicit disapproval in each of the newspaper accounts hints that they were not outwardly bitter. The most unexpected part of the ceremony followed Douglass' speech. The prosecuting attorney Andrew Hunter, who over twenty years earlier had tried and convicted Brown of murder, inciting a slave insurrection, and treason against Virginia, rose to shake Douglass' hand, evidently moved by his portrait of Brown. Hunter remarked that if Robert E. Lee was alive and present that he would be shaking Douglass' other hand.

Storer College provided Douglass the platform from which to speak. Nowhere else in the nation would this speech have been more relevant to the location, the historical figures involved, or to the audience. Douglass was not only one of the great men of the century, he was also a trustee of the college. The symbolism of this speech from this man at this place was a high point in the history of the school.

The legacy of Douglass' impact on Storer can also be traced back to the students' reaction. After Douglass died in 1895 they formed a Frederick Douglass Memorial Association. The college newspaper announced regular meetings with articles and poems inspired by the man they called "an example for coming generations." In May 1895, a student author wrote,

A star has gone out of our sky, whose place must remain in darkness. Others may rise to as great prominence but none can struggle through the clouds as he has done. It is true that Lincoln and Garfield rose from humble surroundings to be presidents, but they had never been crushed by the galling chains of slavery as had our great race leader. Never did we realize so truly, how dear he was to us, until he was taken away from us.

To consider the wider implications of Douglass' 1881 address, connections become apparent. The speech alone represents a breathtaking rate of change that so often goes unacknowledged. Twenty-two years before, at the time of the Brown raid, Douglass' presence as a free man of color speaking about the virtue of a white man attempting to violently free black men would have started a riot akin to John Brown's raid itself. In 1881, such an event produced minimal stir. It spoke to the promise of Storer College. An institution created to educate people of all races, genders, and creeds was the perfect beacon of a more equal and less divided world. John Brown in many ways heralded this promise of Storer. He lived his life to bring about a world where races could coexist peacefully. His violent methods troubled many throughout the years, but his racial ideology has increasingly become the norm in our society. Visitors to Storer's old campus today are still called to think upon the promise of Storer College, the importance of education for all, and John Brown, both his vices and virtues. Perhaps it will always be the responsibility of every generation to think critically about the implications of violence, equality, and education raised by the occasion.

CHAPTER 11

Building Up a Community: The Storer College Role in Expanding Home Ownership

By James Beckman

The 1870 census described twenty-seven-year-old George Weaver as a colored, illiterate farm laborer; by the time of his death in 1918, he was noted as a "very well respected" citizen of Harpers Ferry, a businessman, and owner of several properties around the town. How did this evolution occur? Very simply, Storer College believed in Weaver and backed that faith with a financial investment that empowered this man—and dozens of other African Americans—to realize the dream of home ownership.

Schools are often rightly credited with affecting positive change in the lives of students through obvious traditional means: the transmission of essential knowledge, exposure to the world's great ideas, and practical vocational training. Yet colleges and universities also possess the power to impact the community beyond their gates, both

George Weaver was one of many African Americans who received assistance from Storer College to purchase homes and property. Weaver purchased this three-story stone and brick house on Union Street and lived there until his death. (Photo courtesy of James Beckman)

by strengthening the overall fabric of that community and by improving the lives of individual residents. The time and place in which Storer College was born—a Reconstruction-era southern town still suffering from the ruin of war and the long shadow of human enslavement—afforded ample opportunities to do both. Fortunately, for men like Weaver, the school opted to pursue that broader mission.

"Though it is not the business of a school to furnish homes for the people," explained the *Storer Record* in February 1897, "the management of Storer College has from the first labored to encourage the people to become owners of real estate." Land ownership, tied to notions of power and citizenship since the inception of America, was likely viewed as a powerful way to enfranchise the African American community Storer served. Even today, home ownership continues to be considered a critical element of the "American dream."

However, the leadership of Storer College went beyond vaguely encouraging people to become homeowners. The school directly assisted fifty African Americans in securing their own homes. As the 1897 *Record* article pointed out, "the Principal of the School has during the past thirty years deeded property, ranging from one-fourth of an acre to eight or nine acres each." The properties, positioned around Harpers Ferry and the adjacent village of Bolivar, were all deeded "in fee simple though a few of them have since mortgaged their property to other parties to get money to build or enlarge their buildings."

The school's benevolence reached beyond its alumni. Of those listed in the 1897 *Record* article, less than one-third were Storer graduates. Certainly a number of these individuals were parents of students or were connected to the school in some other fashion. For example, one beneficiary was listed in the 1880 census as a domestic servant of a Storer trustee. Another was listed in the 1900 census as President McDonald's boarder, as well as a cook at the Lockwood House Hotel on campus. However, many of the people receiving this assistance had no significant prior connection with Storer College at all and were merely individuals whom the school's leadership thought worthy of help.

These personal, life-changing transactions were instrumental in strengthening the broader community as a whole, instilling in those with the most humble beginnings the confidence to participate in political and business affairs. Of the forty-two individuals listed as receiving assistance from Storer in 1897, thirty were male, and thus eligible to vote and help shape the future of their town, state, and country. Two-thirds of these men were indeed listed as registered voters by 1892, while at least six were involved in local and state politics, and some were even running for office. The most notable of these was Hamilton Hatter, who in 1892 became the first African American to receive a regular party nomination for the West Virginia legislature. Hatter went on to become a professor himself at Storer College and later served as the President/Principal of Bluefield State College from 1895-1906.

George Weaver, born and raised in Virginia during the era of slavery, was noted in 1867 by the *Spirit of Jefferson* newspaper to be attending "secret" meetings with Nathan Brackett, the future principal of Storer College. Likely, Brackett was attempt-

ing to educate Weaver about the new school in Harpers Ferry and gain his support. Years later, Weaver would take advantage of that school's homeownership program to purchase a three-story stone and brick house on Union Street in Bolivar. He would live in this home with his family for the next half-century and make improvements to the lot, again with Storer's assistance. In the 1880s, he also built a modest wooden frame structure in Harpers Ferry on the corner of Washington and Boundary Streets for his son, James Weaver. In the ensuing years, George Weaver developed a thriving ice harvesting business and acquired additional properties along the Shenandoah River for this purpose. He became a member of the Board of Trustees of the John Wesley Colored Methodist Church, served for many years as Superintendent of its Sunday School program, and directed

Hamilton Hatter (History of American Negro, Vol. VII, West Virginia)

the church choir. Following his death, his obituary lauded him as a "very well respected" citizen of the town. He died at his home on Union Street—the very same house Storer College had helped him purchase and improve so many years before.

While women's suffrage would not be recognized until the ratification of the Nineteenth Amendment in 1920, one can easily imagine the empowerment this program offered its twelve female beneficiaries. In a world where gender, marital status, and color often limited opportunities for lending, this chance to own one's own home must have been deeply appreciated by the women.

Throughout the life of the school, Storer College would continue to seek ways to benefit the community beyond its gates. From giving students clothing, temporary lodging, and other fundamentals in the early years, to creative financial aid and employment opportunities during the Great Depression, the school did what it could to provide financial assistance—even though the school was always very hard-pressed itself for resources. President Henry T. McDonald reported to the Storer College Board of Trustees in 1933 that he was doing everything possible to help students and that "we secured some financial assistance from alumni and friends, we made liberal scholarship grants, whenever possible we created jobs, wherever there was the slightest excuse." Ultimately, the school's own funding struggle would be a leading cause of its closure; however, its generous commitment to African American home ownership was an investment with priceless, unfathomable returns.

CHAPTER 12

Brave Spirits: The Lovetts of Harpers Ferry

By Catherine Baldau with Cynthia M. Gayton

"Mr. Lovett has built a hill-top house in a lovely place. It is filled in the Summer time, while he has music for the boarders. That makes it pleasant during the warm weather of the Summer months, and it is one of the loveliest places that can be found on the B. & O. Railroad, and the white people go their [sic] from all parts."

—Kate Drumgoold, 1898

In her autobiography, *A Slave Girl's Story*, Kate Drumgoold never mentioned Storer College by name when she described her school in the Blue Ridge "where the very air of heaven seemed to fan the whole hill sides, and there never was a more lovely place on this earth for one to learn a lesson, for we could see the key to all lessons where nature had designed for a grand school of learning."

Storer College, founded in 1867, served for nearly ninety years as a gateway for African Americans striving to enter the ranks of middle-class America. Kate Drumgoold was one such example and in her writings she introduced to the wider world, the Lovett family. Like Drumgoold, they came out of slavery, worked hard, believed in education, became successful entrepreneurs, and were emblematic of the rise of an African American middle-class.

Of the Lovett family, Ms. Drumgoold wrote:

> Mr. William Lovett is one of the finest gentlemen anywhere around the whole country, and is much beloved by all who know him…. He has a large family of girls and boys and all are smart. He sent two of them to the Hillsdale College when they had finished at the Ferry, and one was John Lovett, who studied law, and the other one, Miss Etta Lovett, was a fine school teacher and a music teacher.

Lovett family anecdotes, newspaper accounts, and legal documents trace their accomplishments. They were achieved under challenging circumstances, which stemmed from racial divisions along the color line, and make them a particularly remarkable family. Most notable, Thomas Lovett, the second of three sons, built one of the most recognizable structures in Harpers Ferry, which happened in great part because of the family's ties to Storer College.

This story of the Lovetts begins in slavery and from the start, women played a crucial role in the family's eventual success. Around 1805, Marcia Blue (also identified as Martha Blue in legal documents) was born into slavery in Virginia. The will of Sarah Opie Parker dated February 2, 1821, emancipated Marcia, while another will initialed by her purported white father, Hiram Lindsey Opie, gave her property and income.

(1) Uncle Tom Lovett. (2) Aunt Etta Lovett (3) Uncle
John Lovett. (4) Miss C, Franklyn (Later Mrs Cook)
(5) Dr. N. C. Brocket (6) Mrs Bracket (7) Mrs Lightner
(8) John C. Newman (9) Jared M. Arten.

Some members of the Lovett family identified in this photo taken at Storer College, including Thomas, Henrietta (Etta), and John. Also pictured: Rev. and Mrs. Brackett (center) and Coralie Franklin (center, striped dress), a contemporary of the Lovetts.

Notably, Hiram Opie did not identify Marcia Blue as a servant in his will, a description he gave to the other "undisposed servants" willed to his four children.

Marcia Blue married Fairfax Weaver and had two children, Sarah Elizabeth Weaver and James Weaver. In 1848, their daughter Sarah married William C. Lovett in Winchester, Virginia. Lovett was a fireman on the Valley Branch (also known as the Winchester Branch) of the B&O Railroad. Together they had eleven children, including three sets of twins. One twin, born during the Civil War, did not survive. The 1870 U.S. Census Record lists them as: Sarah (Mary in 1860 Census), James, Elizabeth (Martha, 1860), Rebecca (Sarah, 1860), Thomas S., John P., Julia V., Henrietta "Etta," Marguretta "Maggie," and Florence. (Note that some names differ from the 1860 census; all of the children are recorded as mulatto, or of mixed race.)

In the second year of the Civil War, the Lovett family, including Marcia Weaver (her husband, Fairfax now deceased), followed "General Banks' retreat of the Union Army" to Pennsylvania. The Union army took possession of their wagon, stranding the whole family, which at the time comprised parents, a grandmother, and eight children. The Lovetts eventually made it to Chambersburg, Pennsylvania, and spent four years there while the Union army confiscated their Winchester property and used the family home as a hospital. The Lovetts returned to the South after the war, and between 1870 and 1880 settled in Harpers Ferry, where they began a lengthy and personal relationship with Storer College.

During this period in the school's history, Rev. Nathan Cook Brackett, president of Storer, helped several African Americans acquire property in Harpers Ferry. Marcia Weaver, already an experienced land owner (and perhaps with assistance from Brackett) purchased a lot on Fillmore Street, across from Rev. Morrell's House. While several Lovett children enrolled in the school, Sarah and William were employed by Brackett to run the boarding operation in the Lockwood House, a building owned by the college. The building had been used for summer boarding since the mid-1870s. A third floor with a Mansard roof was added ca. 1883, providing ten more rooms and making the Lockwood House a busy hotel.

As their parents' business thrived, the Lovett children and grandchildren attended and/or worked at Storer, became homeowners, and met and married spouses. On March 3, 1897, Rev. Brackett married Florence Lovett to James Monroe Canty, an instructor at the West Virginia Institute and alumnus of Booker T. Washington's Tuskegee Institute. The *Washington Post* reported their marriage in the March 29, 1897, column, Colored American Notes: "Mr. J. M. Canty, in charge of the industrial department of the West Virginia Institute, recently married Miss Florence Lovett, of Harper's Ferry. Miss Lovett is the youngest daughter of a family which almost monopolizes the hotel facilities of Harper's Ferry."

Regardless of other successes, the Lovetts were best known as hoteliers. Mary Brackett Robinson remarked on the success of the Lockwood Hotel, "Every evening throughout the season the family used to gather around the piano and entertain their guests and themselves with singing. The piano stood in the big hall and the porches were filled with appreciative listeners." In her history of the college, Kate Anthony wrote:

> Camp Hill, which had previously been like a graveyard in the summer, has become the center of life in the town, having all available rooms filled to overflowing with an excellent class of summer boarders. Several hundred guests come annually, and the number increases every year. This gives business to the town, and employment to a considerable number of students, while guests are sure of having intelligent, honest and faithful attendants.

When William Lovett died in 1888, Sarah continued to run the business with assistance from her children—James as chef, and Thomas as hotel clerk. In this era

Interior view of the lobby of Lockwood House Hotel, ca. 1900. Boarders could post letters and postcards using the cast iron mailbox on the counter. Note the kerosene wall lamp on the right and lantern on the wall above the mailbox. The family and guests gathered around the piano for lively summer evenings.

Harpers Ferry became a prime summer and weekend destination, especially for urban African Americans who sought respite from the heat of the city in a location of historical significance. In his study of this period, historian Andrew W. Kahrl wrote,

> Though their leisure activities might at first glance seem unremarkable, their choice of location, the meanings they invested in such pursuits, and their critique of each others, reveal a heretofore unexplained dimension of the broader contest over the memory of John Brown and the reality of Jim Crow.

Thomas Lovett recognized the appeal of Harpers Ferry as a destination for blacks and whites. With the Lockwood House consistently booked to capacity, Thomas and his wife Lavinia Holloway Lovett opened the Brackett House, another college building, to accommodate the overflow of guests. Lavinia Holloway was born in New Bern, North Carolina, in 1855 and graduated as a nurse from the New England Hospital for

Women and Children in 1881. The couple had two daughters, Florence and Charlotte. According to Kate Drumgoold, "Mr. Thomas Lovett is a school teacher and very much beloved. He married a doctress, who is one of the finest ladies that lives."

With Thomas now overseeing operations at the Brackett House, his sister Maggie and her husband Allen P. Daniel assisted Sarah Lovett with the daily operation of the Lockwood. Around this time Thomas Lovett conceived a bolder plan. Standing atop Magazine Hill, where the former U.S. Armory stored the gun powder of its arms-making factory, with a commanding view of the confluence of the Potomac and Shenandoah rivers, Lovett purportedly proclaimed, "Here, where the martyrdom of John Brown took place, is where I will build my hotel."

Local newspapers tracked the hotel's progress. The May 7, 1889, *Spirit of Jefferson* announced, "Tom Lovett is fencing the Magazine Hill lot and is about to build. He had been a pioneer in entertaining summer guests and deserves success." The *Harpers Ferry Sentinel* described the hotel on January 22, 1890, as a "frame building with 25 rooms to cost between $3,000 & $4,000. Expected to open next summer." And the May, 14, 1890, *Virginia Free Press* reported, "Hilltop House of T. S. Lovett on Magazine Hill HF almost completed. He has enviable reputation as host. View from hotel is beyond description."

The hotel almost immediately became the success that Thomas Lovett envisioned. He hired Storer students to help manage the business. The *Storer Record* boasted, "T. S. Lovett, class of '76, has built a fine summer house on 'Magazine Hill' and is one of the leading hotel men at Harper's Ferry." Continual upgrades and additions made the Hilltop a remarkably modern and luxurious hotel. Amenities soon included electric lights, bath tubs with hot and cold running water, a dance pavilion, and 4,000 square foot dining room. On a return visit to the Ferry in 1895, Storer alumnus Kate Drumgoold wrote:

> I had the pleasure of stopping there on my way home…and it did my soul good to find such a fine house built by one of the colored gentlemen and one that I had known; for I was at his mother's boarding house for the whole time that I was at the Ferry. He was teaching school then in the Winter time and looking after his mother's business in the Summer time. So I am glad that some of my people are trying to make an honest living. He is one among the many at the Ferry that are keeping boarding houses; and I am thankful for all that comes to us as a race.

By 1904, the Hilltop House operated year-round. Lovett installed a steam-heating plant to keep his guests comfortable in the winter months. A fire in December 1912 destroyed the western portion of the hotel, but Lovett rebuilt in time to receive guests the following summer. Congressmen and other Washington dignitaries often made the short excursion to Harpers Ferry. In 1915, the Hilltop Hotel even hosted the President of the United States. The *Washington Post* reported on October 17, 1915:

The "Hill-Top House," and Ridge street, west

Postcard showing a street view of the Hilltop House on Ridge Street in Harpers Ferry, West Virginia, ca. 1908. W. L. Erwin, photographer.

It was raining and the roads were muddy, but the holiday makers were not to be discouraged, and noon found the White House car at Harpers Ferry, 72 miles away. At an inn overlooking the Potomac and Shenandoah rivers the President registered, writing "Woodrow Wilson and party."

Hill Top House is run by Thomas Lovett, who took the greatest pleasure in escorting the party over the hotel, taking them on to the great balcony, where can be seen the beautiful country for miles around, including numerous points of historical interest. It happened that it will be 56 years today since the famous John Brown started his raiding at Harpers Ferry.

A *New York Times* article of the same date did not cite Thomas Lovett by name, but stated, "The inn is kept by a negro family."

Another fire in June 1919 devastated the hotel. Despite this tremendous loss, Lovett, who by now had proven himself to be undeterred by setbacks, immediately began plans to rebuild. Page three of July 28, 1919, *Washington Post* read, "Thomas S. Lovett has made arrangements to rebuild the Hilltop House at Harpers Ferry which was destroyed by fire several weeks ago. The hotel will be rebuilt upon the old plans, as a considerable part of the foundation can be utilized again. The work is to be begun at once."

An undated brochure for the third incarnation of the Hilltop House—identifying *T. S. Lovett, Proprietor* on the cover—described the view as well as the luxurious accommodations available to those who journeyed to the historic town:

Amid the rugged mountains of West Virginia, made historic by the thrilling adventures of John Brown and his band of fanatical followers, Harpers Ferry offers to the wayfarer seeking health and recreation more of interest than any spot in America. Here the Potomac and the Shenandoah mingle their waters, offering to the sportsmen the ever new joy that attends the rod and reel.

The old Hill Top House, destroyed by fire December 11th, 1919, has been replaced by a new stone building provided with every modern convenience, including long distance phones....

All who have sought rest in this mountain Inn have discovered that somewhere there is a guiding mind always alert to cater to their well being. The sleeping chambers with their characteristic freshness induce slumber. Time that might hang heavily upon idle hands is beguiled by music and games. Three thousand feet of verandas, two hundred and fifty feet above the rushing waters of the majestic streams, affords promenades and lounging places. There one may watch the speeding trains as they pass along what appear, from the lofty heights, to be miniature railways.

Thomas and Lavinia Lovett continued to operate the hotel until 1926, the year that two of Tom's siblings, James and Louise, died within months of each other in Harpers Ferry. The Lovetts sold the hotel and moved to New York where they lived with their daughters and a son-in-law. Thomas died in Harpers Ferry on July 13, 1940, and Lavinia died in New York in 1944. Florence Lovett Martin died on October 16, 1963, in Harpers Ferry, where she had lived since 1960, and Charlotte, the last Weaver-Lovett descendant to bear the Lovett name, died in Harpers Ferry in 1979.

The Hilltop House was the longest operating hotel in Harpers Ferry until 2008 when it was bought by a property development business. While mostly in ruins, visitors can still see remnants of the structure Thomas and Lavinia rebuilt in 1919. Caretakers do their best to maintain the landscape around the once proud hotel and annex buildings, where an American flag still flies. The success of the Hilltop House Hotel, built by the grandson of a slave and Storer graduate in a period highly charged with discrimination and segregation, is not diminished by the crumbling façade. What African American author G. F. Richings wrote about Harpers Ferry in 1902 is still true: "No one can visit Harper's Ferry without coming away overflowing with wonder and enthusiasm. One stands abashed before the brave spirit, the devotion and never-mentioned sacrifices of our toilers there."

Allen Mercer Daniel

Another member of the Lovett family who achieved high success was Thomas' nephew, Allen Mercer Daniel. Daniel's parents, Maggie and Allen P., continued to operate the Lockwood House Hotel after Sarah Lovett's death in 1911 until it closed in 1926. Allen Mercer Daniel grew up on Camp Hill, among the hills, rivers, and legend of John Brown, a part of the sprawling Lovett family. He attended Storer College and, as a student, helped Joseph Barry edit *The Strange Story of Harper's Ferry* while Barry was living in the Lockwood House. After Storer, Daniel studied at Howard University, earning degrees in business and law. He became the college's law librarian,

Class of 1905 with Allen Mercer Daniel standing tall in the middle of the back row. Daniel's parents, Allen P. Daniel and Maggie Lovett Daniel, operated the Lockwood House Hotel from 1911 until it closed in 1926. A. M. Daniel went on to a have a distinguished career as the law librarian at Howard University.

the first African American member of the American Association of Law Librarians, and in 1971 was present at the dedication of the Allen Mercer Daniel Law Library at Howard University. Also present was one of his former students, Thurgood Marshall, Associate Justice of the U.S. Supreme Court. As a lawyer, Marshall successfully argued the *Brown v. Board of Education* case before the Supreme Court. The 1954 decision desegregated schools, which prompted the West Virginia legislature to withdraw state funding to Storer College.

A successful attorney, educator, writer, and librarian, Allen Mercer Daniel never forgot his roots in Harpers Ferry or the achievements of his family members. He wrote of his uncle's hotel:

> If you were on train No. 5 of the B&O Railroad as it passed through the tunnel under Maryland Heights, over the bridge that spanned the Potomac River and stopped at the station at Harpers Ferry, you would glance to the West and see etched against the sunset sky the Hill Top House. Solid as the Rock of Gibraltar standing as a monument to Thomas S. Lovett.

CHAPTER 13

"The Professor"
Henry T. McDonald

By George Best

A tall man, with a waxed mustache and hair that seems to have only barely been tamed by the comb, Henry T. McDonald stands out in any photograph. And well he should. If a list were to be compiled ranking the most influential people in Harpers Ferry's long and rich history, his spot would be close to the top. McDonald was not only the longest-serving president of Storer College but also served as mayor of Harpers Ferry, became a prominent local historian, and promoted the establishment of Harpers Ferry National Monument, which today, under a slightly different name, continues to preserve the town and college.

Henry Temple McDonald was born on May 9, 1872, in Blue Earth, Minnesota, to James McDonald and Sarah Blanchard McDonald, the fourth of five sons. The early death of James, a Union army veteran, forced the McDonald boys to assume many responsibilities in running the family farm. While he worked hard tending to the cattle and crops, young Henry was an avid student. Devotion to his studies quickly earned him the nickname "Professor" from his classmates, unknowingly predicting what lay in the young man's future. He graduated high school in 1892 as the valedictorian and immediately set his sights on higher education, deciding on Hillsdale College in Michigan. McDonald was apparently swayed to attend Hillsdale after hearing a sermon of "wonderful fire and eloquence" from Rev. Ransom Dunn, a professor at the college and early leader of the Freewill Baptist movement.

Henry T. McDonald served as Storer College president from 1899 to 1944.

"Professor" McDonald continued to live up to his nickname in college. In addition to his academic pursuits, he played football and joined several on-campus organizations in which he frequently held leadership positions. Well-liked by his teachers and classmates, he was chosen to be the editor-in-chief of a school publication and to speak at his graduation. McDonald received his Bachelor of Arts and Mas-

A young Henry T. McDonald (fifth from right) poses with faculty in 1909, a decade after he became president of the college. He would have been in his late thirties when this photo was taken. A long, eventful career still lay ahead for him at Storer. McDonald's wife Elizabeth is to his left.

ters of Arts in 1897 and immediately embarked on what proved to be a long and successful career as a teacher and administrator.

Following graduation, McDonald was the principal of two high schools, North Adams and Hillsdale, both in Michigan, serving in the former for a year and a half and the latter for six months. In the middle of the school year at this last position, he accepted the appointment to Storer College. Now, in 1899, only two years after his graduation from Hillsdale College, Henry "Professor" McDonald would become Professor Henry McDonald.

McDonald assumed his duties as the principal of Storer College for the 1899-1900 school year (the position name interchanged from principal to president). Over the next forty-five years, he saw the college through its greatest period of growth. While Storer had come a long way since its humble beginnings in the Lockwood House just after the Civil War, it was not doing well in 1899. Many of the buildings were in disrepair, "with splintered floors," little to no paint, and otherwise in a state of "impoverishment." There was scant money for repairs, enrollment was dropping, and most classes were only offered at the high school level. Despite these difficult beginnings, McDonald built on the legacy left by Nathan Brackett and others to bring Storer College to its peak and finally, in 1938, make it a four-year degree-granting institution.

In 1906, campus consisted of eight buildings. By 1914, that number had jumped to thirteen. Where enrollment had been low when McDonald arrived, the school reached its numerical peak during his tenure. He fundraised for and purchased John Brown's Fort, moving it from the Murphy Farm to campus in 1909—the 50th anniversary of John Brown's Raid—and converted that humble yet illustrious building into a museum. Henry McDonald came to love Storer College and transformed it into a proud institution.

None of this would have been possible if McDonald did not feel driven to achieve for both the college and himself. He very much believed that his work at the school was a mission in the religious sense of the word, although his goal was not to convert his students to a particular faith. Rather, he saw his mission as one of liberation. Shortly after taking over the principal position at Storer, he told his mother, "There is something fitting in my being here in this work. Father fought and worked for the physical freedom of the colored people and I'm in a way carrying on work he was engaged in by working for their intellectual freedom." In two 1933 letters to potential donors, he stated that the school's mission was "to emancipate the mind and soul of those, whose bodies were freed by the decision of war.... It is conducted as a missionary enterprise." The school, he wrote, was "the natural monument to John Brown" and that it was his mission to continue what Brown and the Civil War had started. He further emphasized this point in a letter to one of Brown's granddaughters, writing, "I

After over forty years of service, Henry T. McDonald (front row, fourth from left) stands proudly with faculty and students from the class of 1942, though WWII had to weigh heavily on his mind. Students barely outnumber faculty in this graduating class of eighteen students, and the devastating effects of the war were only just beginning.

In retirement Henry McDonald continued to work for the betterment of the community. He worked diligently with others to lobby for the creation of Harpers Ferry National Historical Park. McDonald's chair shown in this photo and on page 84 is in the park's museum collection.

always think of this school as carrying into complete effect the plans and ideals of your martyr grandfather." The African American people had attained freedom, but slavery had left them completely bereft of education. It was McDonald's mission, as he saw it, to provide that education to them.

McDonald's mission-oriented approach had its roots in the New England abolitionist movement. While born, raised, and educated in the Midwest, his ancestral ties were to New England and he felt drawn to them his entire life. As noted above, he was also very aware of the legacy upon which he was building left by not only his father, but all of those who had worked for the freedom and education of African Americans. His wife, Elizabeth (née Mosher), was herself the daughter of some of the school's early educators. This New England mission-oriented approach unfortunately lent itself to paternalism in its attitude toward African Americans. While McDonald deeply cared for and respected his students and black colleagues, he exhibited a paternalistic streak himself. While African Americans could work hard, earn education, and gain the respect of white Americans within the racially divided United States, they were clearly still seen as an "other," an attitude that McDonald shared. In his eyes, African Americans could gain his respect but would never quite be acknowledged as his equal.

While McDonald's primary focus and work was with Storer College, he also became involved with the town of Harpers Ferry and its history. It was not long before he established himself as a prominent, local historian. He constantly collected historical paraphernalia, especially items associated with the town, and displayed them at Storer. "My much better half [Elizabeth], says that I have been a junk collector," he wrote an acquaintance. "I confess there is some righteousness in her accusation." McDonald frequently offered lectures on Harpers Ferry and its importance to American history. During a stint as mayor of the town in the 1920s, he saw what he felt was a golden opportunity to rejuvenate Harpers Ferry and make some more history of his own by petitioning Congress, albeit unsuccessfully, to locate the summer home for the President of the United States in Harpers Ferry. He would, however, prove more successful in his efforts to make Harpers Ferry into a National Park. In large part thanks to his efforts, in 1944 Congress passed and President Franklin Roosevelt signed into law an act creating Harpers Ferry National Monument. McDonald was immediately appointed to the committee to plot out what land and buildings would fall within its boundaries, and he chaired the committee in 1947 and 1951.

McDonald's long career as the President of Storer College finally came to an end in 1944. World War II was not kind to the school, which saw its enrollment and staff severely shrink as the men joined the military in droves. As time had passed, McDonald's views on race and education had not kept up. The African American community became especially critical. McDonald's views on race, if compared to an African American thinker, were most in line with those of Booker T. Washington in the early 1900s. An opposing viewpoint pushed by W. E. B. Du Bois that African Americans and whites should be treated equally and fully integrated, ultimately won out, clashing with McDonald's views, and decreasing his popularity in the local black community. In addition, McDonald was aging—he turned seventy in 1942—and there was a general feeling that it was time for a change of the guard. Finally, in the spring of 1944, after forty-five years of service, Henry McDonald submitted his resignation. He died in 1951.

While Storer College closed its doors only slightly more than a decade after McDonald retired, his legacy and impact on the place is still readily apparent. His last major effort, the formation of Harpers Ferry National Monument, now Harpers Ferry National Historical Park, still exists and includes many of the original Storer College buildings. While there was some friction after a time between McDonald and his students, many kept in touch with him and took pride in the fact that they were educated at Storer College under his tutelage. One alumnus, Rev. Joseph T. Holmes, considered it "a real treat" to hear from "Pres. Mack" and was eager to help McDonald in any way he could. While McDonald's legacy is complicated and has its racist blemishes, the overall impact of the five decades he lived in Harpers Ferry was ultimately a positive one. He ensured a quality education was provided to those who were often denied it elsewhere and laid the foundation for Harpers Ferry and its history to be preserved for many generations to come.

CHAPTER 14

The 1906 Niagara Movement at Storer College

By James Koenig

In 1949, the renowned black educator and historian, W. E. B. Du Bois wrote, "Of all the civil rights for which the world has struggled and fought for 5,000 years, the right to learn is undoubtedly the most fundamental." Forty-three years earlier on the campus of Storer College Du Bois, leading a group of civil rights crusaders called the Niagara Movement, demanded this same right. Du Bois later said that the meeting of the Niagara Movement at Harpers Ferry in 1906 was "one of the greatest meetings that American Negroes ever held." The four-day gathering of 150 men and women represented nearly all regions of the country. This was an influential event of its day, and the themes addressed then reverberate across time to the present day.

The Niagara Movement was founded in 1905 at Niagara Falls, Canada, to address racial discrimination in society, the courts, and all levels of government. In addition,

Gathering of intellectual and politically astute Africa Americans at the Niagara Movement meeting at Storer College in 1906. The group was led by W. E. B. Du Bois (front row, fifth from right) with J. R. Clifford, West Virginia's first African American attorney and Storer graduate, seated to his right. Another speaker at the event, Rev. Reverdy C. Ransom, stands in the back row, second from left.

participants sought to develop a strategy to counter a philosophy popularized and espoused by the highly influential black educator, Booker T. Washington. In a famous speech known as "The Atlanta Compromise," Mr. Washington proposed accommodation of Southern paternalism as the path to equality with whites—rather than direct confrontation of racial injustices. Both Washington and Du Bois promoted education as a means of advancement for African Americans, but Washington favored industrial and agricultural education, while Du Bois—the first African American granted a Ph.D. from Harvard—believed intellectual achievement would elevate his race.

At the turn of the twentieth century, Storer College offered courses for both the head and the hands, a liberal arts and an industrial arts education. Students promoted this blend of the opposing philosophies of Du Bois and Washington in their newspaper, the *Storer Record*: "Prosperous people are those who are industrious, economical, and intelligent.... Let us now make some heroic efforts toward achieving results, which will forever be tributes to Storer College.... Let this be your motto, Rely upon yourself."

One Storer graduate who expounded this philosophy was J. R. Clifford, West Virginia's first black attorney. Clifford was also a founding member of the Niagara Movement. When the question of the location of the movement's second meeting arose, Clifford helped Du Bois make arrangements with Storer College President Henry T. McDonald and his staff to hold the meeting on the college's campus. Few places welcomed large gatherings of African Americans, so the buildings of Storer College (mostly vacant over summer break) made this civil rights meeting even more unique.

In addition to being the location of a historically black college, Harpers Ferry had national symbolic value. In 1859, it was the scene of the raid by John Brown who planned to incite a slave rebellion in the hope of ending slavery. He and his band of followers seized the United States Armory at Harpers Ferry but failed in their attempt. Still, the nationwide publicity accompanying Brown's trial and hanging served his cause perhaps far more than the raid itself. Many saw Brown's attack as the opening salvo of the Civil War, though the actual start was eighteen months into the future. To many, the town was the location of deadly folly instigated by a madman and the scene of Civil War. But in the eyes of others, Harpers Ferry became a pilgrimage site honoring the cause of freedom for all Americans. Du Bois summed it up in a postcard announcing the 1906 meeting: "The meeting place is cool, attractive, and teeming with historic interest."

The Niagara Movement's meeting at Storer College took place August 15 – 19, 1906. The itinerary included speeches, meetings, special addresses, and ceremonies. On "John Brown's Day," the Niagarites made a silent pilgrimage to John Brown's Fort, at the time located on the Murphy Farm, approximately two miles from the campus. There, members removed their shoes and socks and marched single-file around the hallowed fort singing "The Battle Hymn of the Republic" and "John Brown's Body."

Reverend Reverdy C. Ransom, DD, an effective and eloquent speaker, gave one of the key speeches entitled "The Spirit of John Brown." African American scholar Dr. Benjamin Quarles regarded the speech as "the most stirring single episode in the life of the Niagara Movement." The president of Storer labeled the address one of the two greatest orations ever given at the school, the other being Frederick Douglass' defense of John Brown in 1881.

Rev. Reverdy C. Ransom, DD (1861-1959)

Rev. Ransom, a minister and bishop in the African Methodist Episcopal Church, used his pulpit to promote the cause of equality for all African Americans. He addressed audiences nationally to champion the establishment of programs that taught self-improvement. His speech in Lincoln Hall at Storer College tackled issues such as: police brutality; an unfair criminal justice system; denial of voting rights and civil rights; a dysfunctional educational system for minorities; and the lack of economic opportunities for African Americans. The Niagara Movement and Rev. Ransom's speech were a clarion call demanding that African Americans receive the same rights and privileges that in principle were granted to all U.S. citizens regardless of race, creed, or national origin.

In "The Spirit of John Brown," Rev. Ransom promoted the notion that John Brown's actions were sanctioned by a higher power. In one passage he wrote, "[John Brown] could not choose his course; the hand of the Almighty was upon him. He felt the breath of God upon his soul and was strangely moved." Ransom portrayed Brown as a prophet-like figure who "believed himself to be sent upon a MISSION UNDER THE AUTHORITY OF HEAVEN," and that "God sent him to Harper's Ferry." (Emphasis is that of Rev. Ransom.)

In addition to biblical references and justifications, Rev. Ransom compared Brown to Oliver Cromwell and Toussaint L'Ouverture, famous historical liberators. Furthermore, he asserted Brown's actions were supported by principles in the founding documents of this country. "He was imbued with the spirit of the Declaration of Independence, and clearly saw that slavery was incompatible with a free republic."

Though acknowledging their mutual goal of equality, Rev. Ransom railed against the philosophy promoted by Booker T. Washington, who widely championed a strategy of accommodation toward white interests before those of blacks. Washington's stance was readily backed by the established political powers, from as high as President Theodore Roosevelt. It was recognized as a strategy that would blunt the collective political bargaining power of African Americans. In his speech, Rev. Ransom argued,

Today two classes of Negroes, confronted by united opposition, are standing at the parting of the ways. The one counsels patient submission to our present humiliations and degradations; it deprecates political activity; ignores or condones the usurpation and denial of our political and constitutional rights, and preaches the doctrine of industrial development while it has no word of protest or condemnation for those who visit upon us all manner of fiendish and inhuman indignities.

What Booker T. Washington and others argued was that African Americans should aspire to gradually become educated and trained as skilled laborers. These "serfs," as Rev. Ransom and others called them would, in effect, be servants to the white race. Only gradually accumulating wealth and property as a subservient class would they eventually gain their full rights as citizens.

One of the founding principles of the Niagara Movement was that African Americans were already citizens and thus should have the rights guaranteed to every citizen under the Constitution. Using "it" to refer to the class of African Americans who demand their full rights, Rev. Ransom forcefully argued,

Founded as this nation is, it does not believe that submission to injustice, the surrender of rights for the sake of an opportunity to labor and save, is the road to the goal of manhood and equality which we seek. It believes the Negro should assert his full title to American manhood, and maintain every right guaranteed him by the constitution of the United States, and having these, all other things will be added.

Perhaps never imagining the full extent to which he was divining the future, Rev. Ransom warned, "Before the strife and hatred of race and class have vanished, many will be called upon to wear the martyr's crown. A new birth of freedom within a nation is always accompanied with great suffering and pain."

Pressing for the need to act while being valiant against detractors, Rev. Ransom invoked a passage from *Hamlet*:

Like the ghost of Hamlet's father, the spirit of John Brown beckons us to arise and seek recovery of our rights, which our enemy, "with witchcraft of his wit, with traitorous gifts" has sought forever to destroy. John Brown was thought by many, even among his friends, to be insane. But an exhibition of such insanity was required to arouse the nation against the crime of slavery and to bring on the Civil War. NO WEAK AND ORDINARY VOICE CAN CALL THE NATION BACK TO A SENSE OF JUSTICE.

The conference closed on Sunday, August 19, with a speech by Du Bois. In "An Address to the Country," Du Bois laid out the Niagara Movement's demands including "full manhood suffrage," an end to discrimination in public accommodations,

Small in numbers but a powerful presence at the 1906 Niagara Movement meeting in Harpers Ferry, these women insisted on equal participation. The Movement's leader, W. E. B. Du Bois, supported their inclusion, but members such as William Monroe Trotter did not. Trotter and a large faction split from the organization in 1908, weakening its influence, but leading to the formation of the NAACP.

equal enforcement of the law, and better education for African American children. His specifics about education clearly defined his differences with Booker T. Washington and echoed the aspirations that were editorialized by students in the *Storer Record*:

> And when we call for education we mean real education. We believe in work. We ourselves are workers, but work is not necessarily education. Education is the development of power and ideal. We want our children trained as intelligent human beings should be, and we will fight for all time against any proposal to educate black boys and girls simply as servants and underlings, or simply for the use of other people. They have a right to know, to think, to aspire.

After the event, one of Storer's leaders, "lady principal" Lura Brackett Lightner, wrote a "very confidential" letter to her brother Nathan, the first principal and founder of Storer. She wrote that "our part of the entertaining has been well done. The people are satisfied, even grateful. But the Movement! I have been in it and not of it." She described the John Brown meeting as "an experience. It must be the culmination of my lessons in sociology. Du Bois and Ransom were the speakers. The addresses were superb. Ransom is a born orator but they are bitter. The poison of coloritis, is it a poison or a leprousy? This leprousy will make these men outcasts if they are not healed."

McDonald corresponded with Du Bois regarding an invitation to host the Niagara Movement again in 1907. McDonald also disagreed with the opinion that the school might lose funding because of its association with Niagara. In 1907, the Niagara Movement met in Boston where they discussed buying land for a permanent home in Harpers Ferry.

Eventually, the Niagara Movement evolved into a much stronger national civil rights organization, the National Association for the Advancement of Colored People (NAACP). Many of the movement's leaders and guiding principles would propel the NAACP to become the most effective civil rights organization of the twentieth century.

It has been over 100 years since the Niagara Movement held its second annual meeting at Storer College and more than 150 years since John Brown's infamous raid. But the call for justice and the struggle for equality continue. The same friction between supporters of the Niagara Movement and the followers of Booker T. Washington continues between progressives and conservatives today, but the hope of W. E. B. Du Bois echoes into this century:

And we shall win. The past promised it, the present foretells it.... Thank God for all those today, few though their voice be, who have not forgotten the divine brotherhood of all men, white and black, rich and poor, fortunate and unfortunate....

Courage, brothers! The battle for humanity is not lost or losing. All across the skies sit signs of promise.... Everywhere the laborer, with ballot in his hand, is voting open the gates of opportunity and peace.... We must not falter, we may not shrink. Above are the everlasting stars."

CHAPTER 15

The Preservation of John Brown's Fort at Storer College, 1909 to 1968

By James Koenig

arpers Ferry, with its glorious mountain and river views, quaint train station, stately buildings and bucolic grounds, is today the home of a national historical park. In Lower Town, near the point where the Shenandoah and Potomac rivers

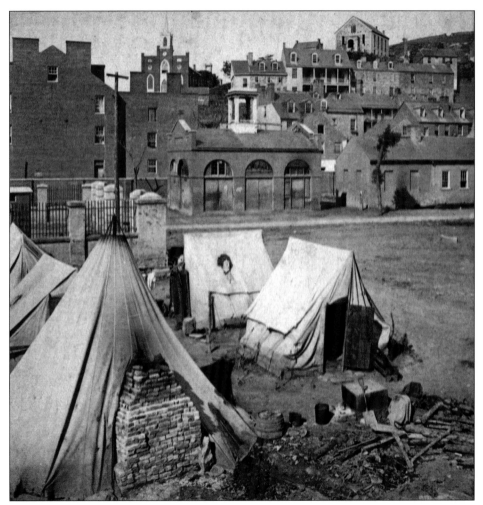

Originally built as the guard and fire engine house for the U.S. Armory in 1848, the building became known as John Brown's Fort after the infamous raid in 1859. This 1865 photo shows the Fort in its original location near the gated entrance to the armory grounds (left). Contraband tents are in the foreground.

converge, sits a modest brick building with a white cupola. Built in 1848, it housed firefighting equipment and served as guard quarters for the sprawling U.S. Armory manufacturing compound. In 1859, the small structure became the flashpoint where the question of slavery would no longer be left to simmer.

On the night of October 16, 1859, abolitionist John Brown and his band of raiders seized the U.S. Armory and Arsenal and other strategic buildings in Harpers Ferry in an attempt to incite a slave rebellion. After several pitched battles with citizens and militia, the raiding party retreated to the fire engine house with a group of hostages. In this small building, Brown made his famous stand against slavery. A contingent of U.S. Marines led by Lt. Col. Robert E. Lee arrived by train from Washington, DC, and on the morning of October 18, stormed the engine house, captured Brown and his raiders, and freed the hostages. Six weeks later on the morning of his execution, John Brown penned these prophetic words: "I, John Brown, am now quite <u>certain</u> that the crimes of this <u>guilty</u>, <u>land:</u> <u>will</u> never be purged <u>away</u> but with Blood. I had, <u>as I now think</u>, <u>vainly</u> flattered myself that without <u>very much</u> bloodshed it might be done."

In retrospect, John Brown's failed raid marked the turning point from peace toward the Civil War. The engine house where he made his famous stand was almost immediately christened John Brown's Fort. It became a symbol for the struggle to end slavery and a magnet for admirers, revilers, and curiosity seekers alike.

The Fort has been moved to four different locations, beginning in 1891 when a group of businessmen concocted a scheme to capitalize on the Fort's fame. They reconstructed it at the World's Columbian Exposition in Chicago, where they charged admission to view it. There, the Fort saw eleven people in ten days. The resulting financial disaster nearly led to the complete loss of John Brown's Fort. Abandoned as a pile of bricks and lumber, at the very last moment a heroine arrived. Kate Field, an accomplished newspaperwoman, lecturer and author, led a campaign to rescue the remains of John Brown's Fort and return them to Harpers Ferry. However, a railroad embankment now covered the Fort's original site. Eventually a deal was struck to erect the building on the Murphy Farm, just outside Harpers Ferry. The Murphy's were promised modest compensation for this arrangement, but sadly Ms. Field died suddenly before the project was fully realized.

Though finally reconstructed on the farm in 1895, the fate of the Fort was once again in doubt. Enthusiasm and funding for the project had sharply declined with the death of Ms. Field, and the once-popular tourist attraction now suffered from a change in the nation's attitude toward the days of slavery and John Brown's Raid. Essentially enough time had passed since the Civil War that the perception of the horrors of slavery had faded, and some prominent historians began to portray the South in a more favorable light.

With this changing perspective, many viewed the symbol of the quest to end slavery with some ambivalence. John Brown's Fort no longer drew the amount of tourists it once had. Without compensation for maintenance, the Murphy family closed the Fort to its few (mostly African American) visitors. The humble engine house that had risen to international fame now stored grain.

John Brown's Fort as reconstructed on the Murphy farm near Harpers Ferry, ca. 1908. Initial enthusiasm for making the Fort a tourist attraction waned and the promise of payment to the Murphy family to maintain and operate the Fort never materialized. Grass, weeds, and prickly bushes eventually overtook the field surrounding the Fort. By the time it was sold to Storer College, the historic building was being used for grain storage.

Once again fate came to the rescue. John Brown's heroism had not diminished in the African American community. They had come from all over the country to visit the Fort in honor of his memory. On a nearby hill overlooking Harpers Ferry, stood the campus of Storer College, with a student body comprised mostly of African Americans. As early as 1899, college president Henry T. McDonald realized the importance of saving the Fort. He actively promoted moving it to the campus since, as he wrote to alumni, it was far more than just a brick building: "From an ordinary engine house it has been transformed into a new Cradle of Liberty."

The college wanted the Fort and the Murphy family offered it for a relatively modest $900. But the college was barely surviving financially and had meager resources to purchase the Fort and move it to the campus grounds. In response to McDonald's persistence, the college community and its alumni rallied to raise the needed funds to purchase the Fort in 1909—the 50th anniversary of John Brown's Raid.

From early on, McDonald envisioned it foremost as a shrine for African Americans, but also as a museum that could enhance the image of the college and, with more people visiting the campus, give Storer greater visibility and boost the number of applicants. He hoped this new image would increase donations and funding for the college.

John Brown's Fort next to Brackett (old Lincoln) Hall. The white rectangle on the building, a marble tablet, was a gift from alumni in 1918 commemorating John Brown's Raid. From the start, President McDonald intended that the Fort be used to house a museum for the display of "any miscellaneous curios which would be helpful to students and interesting to tourists who might visit the school."

It's not clear when the museum officially opened, but the 1913 college catalog reported, "The John Brown Fort is being fitted up as a museum…we have the beginning of a mineralogical collection (and) curios from that distant land (India)." An article in the May 1913 issue of the college newspaper, *Storer Record*, described the building being readied for visitors with "the reception of geological, botanical and all other specimens of interest." A college treasurer's report noted, "The museum grew slowly, a book here and an artifact there, mostly donated through personal effort of Dr. McDonald in correspondence with friends of Storer College."

Once the museum opened, staff, alumni, and friends from across the country began to send curios for display. Alumni serving overseas during WWI sent war relics and souvenirs including a variety of helmets, a fragment of a German airplane, and two machine gun bullets.

A 1919 issue of the *Record* reported, "Additions to the Museum are made frequently and we feel sure as time goes on, these will be a rare collection of souvenirs and curios." In 1920, the newspaper mentioned, "Mrs. Cooper of Bolivar Heights, now in Alaska, has our thanks for some interesting samples of gold from that far off land of riches." The report continued, "Wm. Laws remembered the museum with some specimens of coral and other things…."

Because it wasn't heated, the museum was open only during the summer months and fall weekends, but the popularity of the Fort and museum continued. This steadfast interest is indicated by a 1926 college newspaper article announcing, "A pamphlet of John Brown and Harpers Ferry is now on sale at the college…. Large numbers of tourists keep coming to visit the college and particularly to see the Fort. Some Sundays there are literally hundreds on the grounds."

In 1927, the ongoing stream of visitors prompted the installation of a way-finding sign as reported in the college newspaper: "The marker made possible by the united effort of the Summer School of last year was placed at the right side of the road, leading out to the memorial gateway. It is a granite block, costing $65.00, on which is inscribed—John Brown's Fort, with an arrow pointing toward the building."

The high visitation to the Fort and museum required someone to be on duty when it was open. The December 1929 *Storer Record* reported, "During the summer, Stewart Payne was the 'official guide' of Storer College. With a badge marked 'John Brown's Fort' he had the air of authority and what history was lacking in written form, he made up and dispensed on the spot!"

The 1946 catalog indicates the museum still remained a pride of the college, noting, "[The Fort] houses relics of the Civil War, early American original patents, the Spanish American War and World War I relics." Elsewhere in the same catalog was an expression of the enduring regard African Americans held for the Fort: "The attack [John Brown] made on slavery at this time sharpened the issues more than ever before, and served no little to hasten the conflict which resulted in the abolition of slavery in America." One respondent to President McDonald's fundraising appeals wrote, "The debt and love and gratitude we owe to that man and the shrine he reared to liberty and enduring happiness cannot easily be discharged in a single generation. And I imagine each succeeding one will count it a privilege to claim that debt a heritage." Another donor wrote, "Our race should always honor him."

The museum in the Fort remained open until the college closed in 1955. In a 2014 interview one of the student guides, Margaret Jackson Smelley, described her experiences working at the Fort during the school's final two seasons. She told of greeting visitors from all over the world, collecting the dime admission fee, and selling souvenirs such as a brief printed history and pictures of John Brown.

After five years of deliberation, in 1960 the Storer College Board of Trustees agreed to sell the college buildings

Interior view of the museum from the second floor. Glass cases on the ground floor exhibited a diverse collection of donated objects, though few had any connection to the Fort or John Brown's Raid.

Students posing with an instructor on the lawn of Anthony Memorial Hall with the Fort in the background. A few scholars have claimed that when the Fort was re-erected at Storer in 1909, the fire engine and guard's quarter's bays were reversed from their original position. While the bays were reversed, it was done in 1895 when the Fort was reconstructed on the nearby Murphy farm and simply copied when the Fort came to the campus.

and grounds to the National Park Service. The campus was eventually repurposed for NPS educational programs and training, thus preserving the story of Storer College for future generations.

From the beginning the National Park Service decided the building would not be used to display the Storer museum collection. Consequently, the trustees sought to return objects on loan and arranged for the remaining artifacts to be sold at public auction.

A local newspaper auction announcement, dated October 13, 1960, listed an extensive and eclectic compilation—a true cabinet of curiosities—such as: Hebrew scrolls, rock specimens, Civil War relics, WWI helmets, a piece of metal frame from the dirigible *Shenandoah*, a small bull whip, slave irons and collar, a Mexican sword, numerous brass figurines from India, old ice skates, wooden shoes, an African fish trap, quill pens, a primitive stone lamp, about forty U.S. patent models, and a sword made from shark's teeth, along with others too numerous to list.

Curiously enough, there were no original John Brown relics, only a replica of John Brown's Fort and a hand-painted picture of the Fort. The former museum docent, Margaret Smelley, remembered a bust of John Brown on display, but its disposition is unknown.

In 1968, the National Park Service moved the Fort one more time to its present place of prominence near its original site. For fifty-nine years John Brown's Fort had found refuge on the Storer College campus. It not only survived but thrived as a focal point of the campus and its mission. College staff and alumni honored and protected the Fort when neglect of the wider world might have left it to ruin. They kept this symbolic flame of liberty glowing until once again it could be rightfully honored as a national historic treasure, a stark reminder of the struggle for freedom and civil rights.

CHAPTER 16

Storer College: On the Path to God Above

By Melinda Day

In 1910, eighteen-year-old Ernest Lee Smith from Craigsville, Virginia, and four-teen-year-old Ora Belle Mitchell of Elkins, West Virginia, each packed for their move to Storer College. The college catalog provided advance instruction of what to bring to school: "A bible; A toothbrush; Three towels; Brush and comb; Three table napkins; Umbrella; Bedding; and rubber shoe galoshes." Expectations of their new lives as students was also explained in the school's catalog: "Education is of more value to humanity when permeated with the spirit of the teachings of Jesus... it has always exemplified in its faculty and instruction a high type of religious life. To that end an active Christian life is encouraged."

Storer, founded and administered by Freewill Baptist missionaries, often meld-ed compulsory student events with religious teachings. These included a national collegiate day of prayer, school competitions to encourage students to read their fa-vorite bible passages, and attendance at church services offered on several occasions throughout the week. Parents were cautioned to observe the Sunday Sabbath and to transport students to dormitories on other days of the week, not on Sundays, because, "We desire to keep the day holy unto the Lord."

The 1910 *Storer College Catalog* also contained an official list of college-sanctioned social events for proper ladies and gentlemen. These events offered opportunities to

Ernest Lee Smith, Class of 1914. (Photo courtesy of Smith's descendant Marvin Greer)

develop the social deportment needed to nav-igate an African American student body nes-tled in a small West Virginia town during the Jim Crow era. The community's acceptance of Storer College was minimal, and life outside Storer's walls was segregated to the standard of the time. The college catalog instructed young students not to accept invitations to social functions in the community, especially during the academic term.

Despite the restrictions of the outside world, Ernest and Ora Belle learned to thrive inside the bubble of Storer College on Camp Hill. The two youngsters arrived with a zest for literature, public speaking, nature, music, language, and performance. They attended all required school events and were often active participants. They sang, recited bible verses, appeared in plays, performed in the brass band,

Storer College band, 1914, with Ernest L. Smith (second row, second from left) and Ora Belle Mitchell (second row, fourth from right).

and wrote articles for the school newspaper, the *Storer Record*. Ernest entered a *Record* essay contest on "The Advantages of a Well Kept Campus and How to Secure It." The prize: one dollar. The *Record's* editor wrote, "After some consideration the award was made to Ernest L. Smith. Apparently the ancient and honorable family of Smith is not dispossessed of all ability to do things well, as shown by the above results."

Later, in his senior year, Ernest wrote another *Record* article proclaiming the wonder of birds. Such written keepsakes of his college years reveal Ernest's talent for creating beautiful images with words. Whether this gift was entirely homespun or inspired by exposure to other poets, "Birds" demonstrated Earnest's ability to spin metaphors and phrases effectively, to transport his readers to a vision of nature that seemed like heaven on earth.

> If we could but be constrained to let our souls take its wonted course for a while to seek out and dwell upon nature and her wonderful works, her generous provisions and the beautiful things that we enjoy, it would be readily seen that among these, birds are one of the greatest gifts to man. The fowls of the air are among the first of God's great creations, nor have they been less deservant of his great and farsighted wisdom in the habitation of the earth…. Yet there is more to be considered than this. Think of a world without birds.

Think of the coming spring with all of its lovely flowers, budding trees, the whisper of its fragrant breezes mingled with the babbling of the little brooks and streamlets without the little song birds, without their beautiful plumage and enchanting songs and melodies to crown such an outburst of nature's grandeur. Such a spring is inconceivable.

Therefore we owe much to the little birds and we should show our appreciation in the care and protection of them. A provision for their care and protection has been made in the government of this country as in many countries and we hope this will be in an international movement as birds as it can be readily seen are one of the man's greatest gifts.

"A light broke in upon my soul
It was the carol of a bird,
It ceased and then it came again." [Lord Byron]

A highlight of Ernest's and Ora Belle's student social life centered on the annual parties hosted separately by the boys and girls of Storer. The parties featured a planned menu as well as musical performances by students and the school band. But perhaps more exciting for the young people, these social conclaves enabled women and men to spend time together, and possibly contemplate whom among the student body could be a suitable future spouse. The annual "Young Ladies Party" was held in Myrtle Hall on March 27, 1914, from seven until ten-thirty p.m. The *Storer Record* reported:

The hall was very prettily decorated, crepe paper, pennants and pictures, flowers and plants were in much evidence…. After the program and been rendered and the menu served, part of the guests retired to the girls dining-room where games were played…decorated with the national colors. The college Band under the direction of their leader Mr. McKenney [sic], furnished music for the games.

The boys were likewise enthusiastic hosts. Of one boys' party, the *Record* said,

Of course it was a success. It always is. The fellows had put life and time and energy into it and their sufficient reward was the often repeated expression of pleasure in the evening's entertainment expressed by their many guests. There was a most enjoyable dignity and evidence of cultured refinement about the whole evening.

Ernest himself had provided a vocal solo at that event.

It is unclear whether Ernest's and Ora Belle's romance began at such a party or elsewhere. Nearby Jefferson Rock, with its scenic view once famously praised by Thomas Jefferson, was a popular off-campus meeting place where one might discover friends, sweethearts, and perhaps future spouses. However, school rules on co-eds were firmly stated to protect the reputations of everyone involved:

> Under no circumstances are young ladies to leave the college grounds after 5 p.m., or to be out of their own rooms without permission except to attend exercise of the school at which teachers are present...[or] to appear at public or other exercise of the school expensively or showily dressed...[or] to have company without permission... [or] to take visitors to their private room without permission from the Superintendent. No student under the age of eighteen years, who is below the 3rd year class, is allowed the company of the opposite sex by special permission.

Ernest and Ora Belle Smith with two of their nine children. The Smiths carried the education and life lessons learned at Storer College with them throughout their lives. (Photo courtesy of Smith's descendant Marvin Greer)

With these regulations governing their conduct, young people had to be creative in pursuing courtship. One Christmas, Ernest delivered a handwritten invitation to Ora Belle, asking her to the college president's house for a party hosted by the president's wife, Mrs. McDonald. Ernest had been studying German, and wrote the invitation entirely in that language. Translated, it read: "E. L. Schmidt would request the pleasure of Miss Mitchell's company at Mrs. McDonald's house, Tuesday evening 8-10 p.m."

On May 27, 1914, Ora Belle and Ernest were married in Harpers Ferry. The very next day, they walked into the Storer College commencement exercises as man and wife. Following graduation, they each moved back to their parents' homes and later reunited as man and wife to begin family life. Ernest registered for World War I and later World War II but was not inducted. The couple settled in Pittsburgh, Pennsylvania, to raise a family of nine children. As Storer College alumni, they followed college news and activities into adult life.

In 1950, Ernest once more put his talented pen to paper and left a small poem in his family keepsakes. His poem recalled his youth, the way he was raised, the mother and God he loved, and a hope that he would meet her again on "The fairy roadway of my dreams, The Path to God above."

Now I lay me down to sleep.
I pray the Lord my soul to keep.
Forever in his loving care
I know that she'll be waiting there
And when the trials of life are o'er
I'll lift my eyes as in day of yore
At the mother's feet this prayer repeat
Now I lay me down to sleep
When I was a little child and knelt at mother's knee
I reveled in the music of a prayer she taught me.
The sweet simplicity of words
The warmth of mothers love
The fairy roadway of my dreams,
The path to God above.

Composed four decades after Ernest's and Ora Belle's enrollment at Storer, the poem demonstrates how the harmony of faith and education encouraged by the school continued to inspire students throughout their lives.

CHAPTER 17

Don Redman
"The Little Giant of Jazz"

By Todd Bolton

"Now you listen to a band like Don Redman. Don's one of the greatest arrangers of 'em all. Yeah, man!"

—Louis Armstrong

In 1916, a child prodigy came to Harpers Ferry to study music. Within a few short years after graduating, this prodigy was universally known as "The Little Giant of Jazz." By the end of his life, he was one of the most influential figures in the history of jazz.

Donald Matthew Redman was born into a musical family on July 29, 1900, in Piedmont, West Virginia. His father, Daniel Redman, was a custodian in the local school and a musician in the Piedmont Colored Band. His mother, Henrietta Walker

A star of the Class of 1920, Don Redman (standing, far left) poses with the baseball team. A well-rounded student and excellent athlete, Redman played not only baseball, but was on the basketball team and the quarterback of the football team.

Class of 1920 with Don Redman on the far right and the college president, Henry T. McDonald on the far left.

Redman, was a music teacher and vocalist. Contemporaries in Piedmont remember Don playing trumpet by age three. He joined his father in the town band at age six and was performing at the Piedmont Opera House before he graduated from high school. In 1915, he graduated from Howard High School, twenty years after his mother had been the first graduate.

In the fall of 1916, Don Redman enrolled at Storer College. An involved and energetic student, his talents extended well beyond music. Along with being in the college band, chorus, and jazz orchestra, he was a member of the college debating society and a regular participant in oratorical competitions. His diminutive size (5 foot 4 inches) did not prevent him from engaging in athletics. He played on the baseball and basketball teams and was the football team's quarterback.

At Storer, Redman was under the musical tutelage of longtime band master, John Wesley McKinney, as well as Charlotte May Nason and Carlotta Stevens Slater, both graduates of the New England Conservatory of Music. Students in the active music department often performed in various locations throughout the community. During Redman's years here, the music students made annual pilgrimages to the Methodist Episcopal Church in Martinsburg and the Wainwright Baptist Church in Charles Town for concerts.

As a student, Redman wrote and performed many original compositions including, "Lilly of the Valley" and "Victory." In 1919, he was one of two juniors awarded the Metcalf Scholarship for academic excellence. That year he also received an honorable mention in the Storer College newspaper for his oratorical offering entitled "The Power of Music." His most lasting musical contribution was the composition of "Alma Mater," which endured for many years at the college.

Don Redman graduated from Storer on May 26, 1920. He played a prominent role in the commencement exercises—singing, delivering an oration, and performing a piano solo. His graduating class was known as the "Peerless Class," which was certainly foretelling for Redman. Upon graduation he didn't forget his alma mater. His love and affection for his college was evident

Redman working on a score in a cramped dressing room prior to a performance.

through his actions. In the spring of 1921, Storer was engaged in a fundraising effort, the "Three Thousand Dollar Drive." Redman returned to Storer with former student Clarence Martin and presented a successful fundraising concert with all proceeds going to the college. During this concert, Redman demonstrated his musical versatility by performing on the piano, clarinet, saxophone, and xylophone.

Redman progressed to advanced work at the Boston Music Conservatory. At that time, he was one of the most highly educated jazz musicians, black or white, in the country.

His professional career started in and around Cumberland, Maryland, not far from his home in Piedmont. In 1923, he traveled to New York with Billy Page's Broadway Syncopators. Soon after, he impressed Fletcher Henderson with his ability to sing, play a multitude of instruments, and arrange with unparalleled skill. Henderson invited him to join his orchestra, and here Redman's career began to flourish.

Redman took all of Henderson's stock arrangements and began completely rewriting them. Being highly proficient with multiple instruments allowed him to compose and arrange using mixed orchestration that harmonized melodies using combinations of instruments from different sections. Louis Armstrong's arrival in the Henderson orchestra provided him additional opportunities. Armstrong was an incredible trumpeter, allowing Redman to arrange in a way that highlighted the vastly talented New Orleans native.

The mid-twenties became an extraordinarily innovative and creative period for Redman. In 1927, Redman accepted the position of leader and musical director for the Detroit-based ensemble, McKinney's Cotton Pickers. Within a short period of time he molded them into a top jazz orchestra that rivaled both Henderson's and Duke Ellington's and made them the star attraction at the Graystone Ballroom in Detroit. The Cotton Pickers eventually became so popular that there was a demand for them to perform outside the Detroit area, although the owner of the Graystone, who was also the financial backer of the band, refused to let them go.

Redman left McKinney's Cotton Pickers in 1931 to form his own band in New York, later stating, "McKinney knew I was getting ready to leave and that I wanted to take some of his men with me." Along with a few of those musicians, he also took Horace Henderson (Fletcher's younger brother) and six members of Henderson's defunct band from Wilberforce College. Redman said, "I barely had the band organized when Irving Mills had gotten me a recording contract with Brunswick." The new band cut its first side before having a trombone section together.

The orchestra became an instant sensation. With his warm and friendly personality, Redman had a great stage presence and the orchestra was wildly popular wherever they played. The Brunswick records they made reflected his brilliance as an arranger unlike anyone else of the period.

Redman usually played saxophone while leading his orchestra, although he was known to sit in for various members of the band in either the brass, reed, or rhythm sections. The *Pittsburgh Courier* noted Redman played "the sweetest soprano sax this side of heaven."

Along with being an innovator and great musician, Redman was an excellent teacher. Band member Harold "Shorty" Baker remembered, "When I joined Don Redman it was just like going to school, with someone like him to sit down and explain things you automatically improved. The way he broke things down you just had to remember. That was the kind of teacher he was. He was a big influence on my musical thinking."

When not on the road, the orchestra was a regular attraction at Connie's Inn in Harlem, New York. They frequently appeared in radio broadcasts and, in 1932, became the first jazz orchestra to have their own radio series sponsored by Chipso laundry detergent. Redman recalled that they were on the air three or four times a week. During this period he also appeared in several films with the orchestra. That same year, Redman wrote original music for the animated short "I Heard," part of the Betty Boop series. The cartoon began with live footage of Redman and the band performing. They made their own Vitaphone short film in 1935 for Warner Brothers called "Sweepstakes."

By the late 1930s, Redman had tired of what he called "the excitement, the bright lights and the star billing," and disbanded the orchestra. In his heart, he wanted to write and arrange full-time, professing that he "liked that part of the business best anyhow." Duke Ellington said, "Don Redman was one of the really great people, a guy everyone loved. He was a great writer and arranger; a forerunner whose ideas have been copied and have re-appeared in various guises right down the line." Throughout his career he wrote and arranged for a host of well-known orchestras including Fred Waring, Harry James, Paul Whiteman, Count Basie, Jimmy Dorsey, and Jimmie Lunceford.

During the early 1940s, Redman continued to get numerous offers to take over bands or organize a new band, but he declined, saying that he wanted to concentrate on his writing. He acquiesced in 1943, putting a band together and recording two sides

Publicity shot of Don Redman, "The Little Giant of Jazz," conducting his orchestra. (Photo courtesy of Todd Bolton)

for V-Disc records that were sent overseas for the enjoyment of American military personnel during the war.

Three years later, in 1946, he was persuaded to go out again for a much larger commitment. Since his reputation and popularity extended well beyond the U.S., he was contracted to organize the first American jazz band to tour Europe since before World War II. With the combination of the war and a recording ban, European jazz fans had been unable to hear any of the new American jazz known as bebop, which had evolved in the early 1940s. It was an adventurous undertaking by Redman. There was no way to know how Europe would react to this dramatic musical revolution. Redman put together an all-star lineup of black and white musicians including trumpeter Peanuts Holland, saxophonist Don Byas, trombonist Quentin Jackson, and pianist Billy Taylor. On September 15, 1946, the orchestra premiered in Copenhagen.

The next day in the Danish newspaper *Land og Folk*, Børge J. C. Møller wrote: "During the war many here in Scandinavia have been believing that our great jazz orchestras were very up to date, but then comes Don Redman and outdoes everything we are able to accomplish on this side of the pond." The tour continued through Sweden, Norway, Belgium, Switzerland, and Germany. Redman recalled, "We did a terrific business all over Europe." Many days they were doing two shows on week nights and three on Sunday to enthusiastic audiences. In Basel, Switzerland, a critic wrote, "No, these were not our guarded Basel people anymore. This was a powerful thunderous eruptive element. The Küchlin Theatre has witnessed storms of applause before, but not to the extent as it happened when Don Redman and his 14 soloists appeared." When the tour concluded in Munich on November 30, the band dissolved, but Redman and a few of the musicians traveled to Paris where the little maestro received a hero's welcome.

Returning home in early 1947, Redman again concentrated his attention on composing and arranging. In 1949, along with Harry Belafonte, he was part of the CBS network's short-lived attempt to showcase black talent with a live weekly musical variety show. In 1951, Redman became the arranger and musical director for Pearl Bailey. He also appeared on Broadway with Bailey in Harold Arlen's "House of Flowers" in 1954 and 1955. In the late fifties, he did small group recordings with Coleman Hawkins, Hank Jones, and Joe Wilder, but never again formed an orchestra. Redman's last national tour in the early 1960s was with the Pearl Bailey Revue. He was in his "customary good form." In his later years the master jazz arranger and innovator rarely performed in public, preferring to work on several extended compositions that have never been publicly performed.

In October 1964, Redman suffered a partial stoke and appeared to be recovering. Then he suffered a second stoke the third weekend in November. Don Redman died on November 30, 1964, at Presbyterian Hospital in New York City. Hundreds attended his funeral at the Walter B. Cooke Funeral Home on 72nd Street. "I think he's the greatest man I've ever known; from a musicians standpoint, from being a musician's musician, from a humanitarian standpoint, from being a gentleman—he's all that," said legendary jazz trombonist, Quentin Jackson. Band leader and jazz drummer Louis Bellson said, "Don Redman was a great force in Music, not only was he a pioneer and a first in many ways, but a great humanitarian…. I hope many people all over the world will have a chance to listen to Don Redman's music because of his remarkable warmth and talent. I feel honored and blessed that I knew such a great man."

In the over half century since his death, Don Redman has remained a revered figure within the jazz community. Leonard Feather, in his *Encyclopedia of Jazz*, called Redman the "first composer-arranger of any consequence in the history of jazz; the first musician with both the inspiration and the academic knowledge for this branch of music." Those sentiments were echoed by jazz journalist Jim Gerard when he wrote that "Don Redman, to a far greater degree than anyone else, created the prototype for the soundtrack to generations of American lives, as generated in nightclubs, films, radio and TV shows." As the *Pittsburgh Courier* said, "Another of the real greats has gone but the contributions which he made will live forever."

CHAPTER 18

Letters from the Trenches:
Storer College Students in World War I

By James F. Horn
Adapted from "World War I and Jefferson County,
West Virginia" (The History Press, 2017)

When the United States entered the First World War in 1917, many Storer College students and alumni enthusiastically signed up to assist the war effort. The president of the college at the time, Henry T. McDonald, ensured that diligent records were kept of the Storer boys who went overseas. He wrote to the men requesting they respond with what service they were doing, as well as a picture of themselves in uniform. By McDonald's own count, 104 sons of Storer served in the armed forces in World War I—102 of these men in the army and two in the navy.

Storer College felt the sting of war early on in America's involvement in the Great War. In the fall of 1917, Daniel B. Newcomer, the eighteen-year-old grandson of Storer's founder, Nathan Brackett, applied for admission into the army's aviation school. He went to Washington, DC, to take an examination and upon passing was sent to a training camp at San Antonio, Texas. Several weeks after he arrived, he contracted measles, which then developed into pneumonia. When Daniel's condition worsened, his parents were notified. They immediately made plans to visit their son. In the midst of traveling to San Antonio, Mr. Newcomer received a telegram that his son had passed. Two weeks later, Daniel Newcomer's body was brought home to Harpers Ferry, and following a service at the Methodist church in Bolivar, Daniel B. Newcomer was laid to rest in the Harper Cemetery.

Commonly during the Great War, students serving overseas sent souvenirs to the school. The objects usually had some sort of significance to the battles taking place in France and became prized possessions of the school. One of the most interesting items obtained by Storer College during this time was

One of the "sons of Storer" who served in WWI.

a silver letter opener. The item came from George C. Blue, husband of Mabel Beasley Blue, who was a Storer graduate, class of 1911. Mr. Blue obtained the letter opener from the house used as living quarters by the Crown Prince of Germany while on the Alsace-Lorraine front in the war, and was "doubtless used by him." All of these objects were displayed in the museum within the John Brown Fort, which was at that time on the Storer College campus.

Perhaps the most popular items sent back to Storer College were helmets. The front line soldiers went out of their way to get German helmets to send home. Robert G. Green sent a German helmet to his alma mater that was described as "a source of wonderment for many, in that it is such a big heavy thing. One might think it large enough for an atlas to wear." Another student with a similar name, Robert P. Green, stated in a letter, "I sent you a German helmet, I hope you received it alright. I will send you something else if I can get it." While serving overseas, Fred Morris reported that when he returned home he would stop by Storer to deliver one of his two German officer helmets to the school's museum. Clarence T. Napper sent over a helmet that was described as follows:

> Another carefully packed helmet came from Sergt. Clarence T. Napper. This too was one captured from a German, or left by him when he went "west" or somewhere else. It showed service. As an object of interest in the museum it will serve a much more humanitarian purpose than it did when it was worn by one who would destroy civilization.

Edgar Snively, who presented the school with the piece of a German airplane, also sent Storer a "Boche" helmet for the museum. Frederick Wims changed things up, however, and sent Storer a blue French helmet that came "with a small French tri-color attached to it, it has been an object of interest to many, while it rested on the chapel piano." All of the items sent to Storer College from her sons were undoubtable evidence that Storer had done her part in supporting the United States in the Great War.

Perhaps even more compelling than the objects sent to Storer College were the letters that Storer's soldier boys wrote to President McDonald. These letters detailed the heartfelt fondness that these men felt for Storer, as well as the vast horrors of war they witnessed. Robert P. Green wrote of his experiences in the 808 Pioneer Infantry Regiment, Medical Corps, American Expeditionary Forces:

> I am glad that I was physically fit for the service, although I have had it tough at times, but that was not long, but I took that like a man and looked forward to the future, for I realize the road to success is not smooth.... I have been in the Verdun and Argonne sector ever since I have been over here. We landed in the Argonne Forest on Sept. 20th, a few days before the drive started. I was under shell fire from the 26th of Sept. until the armistice was signed. My gas mask which was my friend, I kept at an alert position at all times, day and

President McDonald encouraged those serving overseas to send items for display in the John Brown's Fort Museum and elsewhere on campus. They responded by sending a variety of helmets, bullets, a fragment of an airplane, and other curios. (Harpers Ferry National Historical Park Museum Collection, photo courtesy of Eric Long)

night, also my helmet and other necessary things.... I have seen with my own eyes some of the gothic piles, those that remain in the sector where I am, most of which have been damaged.... I have found the French to be a warm hearted and grateful people. They put forth every effort to make it pleasant for a soldier, I know this to be true from contact.

Anthony Y. Lewis served with the 505 Engineer Corps building railroads and other infrastructure projects in France. He wrote this letter to President McDonald following the armistice signing:

One year ago today we first saw the coast of France and at nine o'clock in the morning we dropped anchor at Breast, Dec. 27th, 1918. Many things have happened since then, but I am glad to say that I have passed through all, and can say I was here to watch the American Expeditionary Forces grow from infancy to a full grown man.... My health has been excellent since I have been here, I have only been sick once and then it was mumps and of course I could not keep from getting them when so great a number of the company had them.... I have, as everyone should have, a clean record in my company. I have never been brought up before any of my officers for a reprimand. Christmas this year was not so good as it could have been, yet it could have been worse. I am certain that it was the happiest one that thousands of people over here had celebrated for quite a while. I know that had not the war ended when it did our Christmas would have been much different to what it was. Then we have something to be thankful for.

Clarence I. Upper was one of the last soldiers to respond to Henry T. McDonald's call for letters about their service. In his letter, he talks about the great misdeeds that he witnessed in Europe and how fortunate citizens of the United States should feel:

It was newsy and strong in determination to bring the Hun to strict accountability for his ravage on civilization in general and France and Belgium in particular, too much cannot be said about the cruelties of the Germans imposed upon innocent women and children. To my thinking this is the saddest chapter of the war, disrespect and degeneration of womanhood and the heavy toll and burden placed on childhood living and potential. Every nation in my opinion should be judged or condemned in proportion as it regards and protects its weakest members, womanhood and childhood. The American people can not possibly know and realize conditions as they exist in this part of the world, "things seen are greater than the things heard of." I would love to give my impressions more fully what I have seen and experienced, but being a soldier I must write simply as a soldier, but I hope on my return to be able to teach thereby giving hundreds the benefits of knowledge and experience I gained over here.... I can not express my feeling in words when the name of Storer College is mentioned. She has done so much for me that the only hope of repaying her is to try and live a clean and upright life, a life that will never bring reproach to her fair name. I realize more every day how much I owe to my ideal home training and the heightening and wholesome influence I was taught at Storer, when I see hundreds of my companions less fortunate than I.

Robert A. McNeal (class of 1908) and Maurice Reid (class of 1914) had a war experience unique from other Storer soldiers. These two men served in the 351st Field Artillery, 93rd Division, one of only two African American divisions that actually saw front line combat in the WWI. In the thick of the fighting, their largest action came during the Meuse-Argonne Offensive. Their division's patch was a buffalo, which proudly paid homage to the famous Buffalo Soldiers that came before them.

Only one student from Storer lost his life during the war. Sergeant John Tindley served in Company K of the 813 Pioneer Infantry Regiment. While serving in France, Sergeant Tindley became ill and succumbed to pneumonia on October 3, 1918. His

The new entry to the campus, Soldiers Gate and Alumni Fence, was dedicated during the 1923 commencement exercises. Two stone pillars with iron gates and the flanking fence replaced the original wooden gates and board fence. The marble dedication plaques pay homage to the Storer students who were veterans of the Civil War, Spanish American War, and WWI.

alma mater called him "the one Storer boy for whom a gold star will always shine in our service flag."

The patriotism, service, and sacrifice of Storer graduates during the First World War cannot be questioned. Their contributions are honored on the college gates, with these two inscriptions on a stone tablet:

To the Students of Storer College who fought in the Civil War 1861-1865,
Spanish American War 1898, The World War 1917-1918

May their illustrious example inspire us to a loyal sense of duty to our country.

CHAPTER 19

Dr. Madison Spencer Briscoe

By Emma Dacol

In 1943, the Second World War was in its full and terrible swing, and one of the Allies' largest stores of invaluable medical supplies had come under the control of Adolf Hitler. In the vicious fights of the tropics, soldiers feared the deadly nip of a malaria-laden mosquito as much as the enemy's bullet. It was in this grim moment that the hour of the "bug man" arrived: Dr. Madison Spencer Briscoe, a longtime Storer College science professor and 1924 graduate.

Briscoe was born March 4, 1904, in Winchester, Virginia. He grew up in a quaint, revolutionary-era stone house, which was shared with a large extended family. The household was headed by Briscoe's grandmother, Nancy Ellen Briscoe. She and her daughter, Briscoe's Aunt Belle, worked from the house as washerwomen. Belle's husband and their three children lived there along with the young Briscoe, his mother, Elmira Robinson, and his father, William Lewis Briscoe. The future scientist's mother worked as a private maid and his father, who was deaf, was a cook at a hotel.

Briscoe's adult relatives were literate but had little formal education. Winchester offered a three-room public school for African Americans in a renovated church, but the program concluded at ninth grade, with no public opportunities for further education in the town. Fortunately, Briscoe was able to continue his education at Storer College, where he excelled in music and academics, and participated in the orchestra and athletics. In 1922, he completed Storer's secondary school program and graduated in 1924 with the second class to receive degrees from the new junior college curriculum.

Madison S. Briscoe, a Storer alumnus, returned to teach in 1930, the first professor to hold an advanced degree in the sciences.

After graduation, Briscoe went on to earn a bachelor's degree in 1926 from Lincoln University in Pennsylvania, and then proceeded to Louisiana, where he joined the faculty at New Orleans University. He taught biology and coached the university's athletic teams. It was there that he met his wife, Marie Byers, an instructor of history. They were married in 1929 and returned to Winchester. Subsequently, Madison

Madison Briscoe (standing, left) and the Storer College Class of 1924. President Henry T. Mc-Donald is seated in the middle.

earned a master's degree in Zoology from Columbia University.

In 1930, Briscoe came home to Storer College, where he was the first professor to hold an advanced professional degree in the sciences. His wife taught at the Douglas School, a public school for African Americans in Winchester. The couple believed education was a ticket to a better life, and they were committed to empowering young people through education. Madison Briscoe was especially passionate about encouraging students to pursue careers in the sciences. Throughout the 1930s, he taught secondary and college level courses in the biological sciences. But he also reached beyond the classroom, taking students on field trips in the local forests to identify and collect insects, reptiles, and other organisms. Such activities were warmly recalled by his students and credited for awakening within them a greater appreciation for science and nature.

In 1934, Storer College took a bold step to expand its science education opportunities by offering a pre-medical studies program. Madison was fundamental in designing the curriculum, which included advanced coursework in embryology, histology, and parasitology.

Madison Briscoe was something of a renaissance man. Beyond academics, he sang in Storer's faculty quartet, played violin, organized a community orchestra, coached basketball, and served as president of the alumni association. In addition to his teaching duties, he published a laboratory manual for general biology, a field checklist for the Harpers Ferry area, and several scientific articles.

In 1941, Briscoe resigned from his position at Storer College to teach bacteriology at Howard University in Washington, DC, and to begin further graduate study at Catholic University in parasitology. By the end of that year, the U.S. was engaged in World War II, and as the conflict spread, there was an increasing demand for expertise in medical fields related to tropical disease. In 1943, Briscoe accepted a commission as first lieutenant in the U.S. Army Sanitary Corps. After being promoted to the rank of captain, he conducted an investigation of diseases caused by infection from *S. haematobium*, a blood fluke that passes through snails before infecting humans. Based on this scientific work, he recommended sanitary and educational measures to prevent infections.

Between 1943 and 1945, he also served as commanding officer of the 16th Malaria Survey Detachment of the U.S. Army in Liberia, West Africa. In that position, this "bug man" conducted a survey on insect vectors responsible for the transmission of microorganisms causing a variety of tropical diseases. His research, in general, contributed to the army's effort to help military personnel serving in tropical areas stay healthy. This work was vital to the war effort, as much of the world's supply of quinine—the most common treatment for malaria—had been housed in warehouses in the Netherlands prior to the war. Nazi forces had seized the Netherlands in 1940, leaving the Allies without access to this precious medicine. Research of alternatives was crucial to the Allied victory, and scientists like Briscoe fought hard to meet that challenge.

When the war ended, Briscoe resumed his academic life, earning his PhD in parasitology in 1950 from the Catholic University of America in Washington, DC. His dissertation was based on his wartime field studies addressing malaria. In 1953, a contract between the Department of the Navy's Office of Naval Research and Howard University sent the "bug man" to Egypt to study ticks, fleas, mites, and lice, as well as the transmission of diseases by insect vectors. Later, Dr. Briscoe participated in a China Medical Board Fellowship, which sent him to Central America for studies on leprosy and other parasitic diseases.

Dr. Briscoe stayed involved with the Storer College community during his career at Howard University. In 1951, the Briscoes bought a house in Harpers Ferry. Though Madison and his wife Marie never had children of their own, they were supportive of Storer students, often greeting those who arrived by train and boarding many in their home. Their one condition for students living with them was that they attend church regularly.

Dr. Briscoe was very passionate about the future of Storer College. After the 1954 *Brown v. Board of Education* Supreme Court decision, the West Virginia State Legislature withdrew funding from Storer College. The school closed its doors in 1955, and a majority of Storer's Board of Trustees voted to liquidate its assets. Dr. Briscoe and his colleague, Mary Peyton Dyson, fought to save the school. In 1959, they filed a civil

Dr. Madison S. Briscoe (1904–1995) at work. (Photo courtesy of the Ellsworth Turner Collection, Stewart Bell, Jr, Archives, Handley Regional Library, Winchester, VA)

suit in West Virginia and appealed it to the District of Columbia. Their efforts were ultimately unsuccessful.

Dr. Briscoe continued to lead a distinguished career at Howard University, becoming a full professor in 1962. He taught parasitology and entomology in the School of Medicine. He was a member of several professional organizations including the American Association for the Advancement of Science, the American Microscopial Society, the Biological Society of Washington, DC, the Pennsylvania Academy of Sciences, the Helminthological Society of Washington, DC, the American Society of Tropical Medicine, the Entomological Society of America, and Sigma Xi.

Dr. Briscoe retired in 1981. At Howard, he is fondly remembered as a pioneer in his field and as an excellent teacher who made parasitology exciting and accessible to students. His published research continues to inform parasitologists today and many of his natural history collections reside in the Smithsonian Institution.

Dr. Briscoe died in 1995 at the age of ninety-one. His legacy lives on in the countless students he mentored and the many lives he touched, whether as an academic or a military scientist, whether personally or through a research record, whether at his little college on Camp Hill or in a jungle far, far away.

CHAPTER 20

Nnamdi Azikiwe
From Colonial Subject to President of an
Independent Nigeria

By Eugene Wilkins

"Storer College has another student this season from Nigeria, Africa, a British possession. Mr. Benj. N. Azikiwe arrived last week to take a course of studies at the college."
—*Farmers Advocate*, Charles Town, WV, October 10, 1925

Did Storer College's president Henry McDonald or any of the other faculty in 1925 know that the twenty-one-year-old, tall, muscular young man with the strange sounding name and peculiar British accent and manner just entering Storer would eventually become the first president of an emerging eastern African Republic? Of course not. Neither did the Class of 1925, his teammates or opponents on the track or football field, or in the boxing ring. Nor did the shopkeepers and workmen down the hill in Harpers Ferry. Neither did Azikiwe himself. But indeed, in 1963—nearly forty years later—the Rt. Hon. Dr. Benjamin Nnamdi Azikiwe was elected the first President of Nigeria. Young Azikiwe also did not know the circuitous and arduous route he would take following graduation from Storer in 1927. He did know, however, the equally circuitous and arduous route he had taken to reach Harpers Ferry.

Born November 16, 1904, Azikiwe grew up in near-primitive regions of Nigeria, learning various tribal languages and cultures. His father, although devoted to him, traveled extensively as a civil clerk for the reigning British government and had to shuttle Azikiwe to a number of relatives and schools throughout the country. Young Azikiwe was enrolled in a series of primary and secondary Catholic, Anglican, Methodist, and missionary training schools. As a result of this exposure to multiple teachers, the bright student began his own formulation of beliefs in African Nationalism and racial and human rights.

At Methodist Boys' High School in the Nigerian state of Lagos, a dedicated teacher emphasized the need for Africans to get a

Benjamin Nnamdi Azikiwe as a student.

college education to help Africa gain its independence from European colonial rule. The instructor provided a list of American schools accepting black students. Azikiwe applied to Storer College, but first this government clerk's son had to find funds to travel to and live in America.

After high school graduation, Azikiwe clerked briefly in the Treasury Department of the British Colonial Service. When he received notice from Storer College President Henry McDonald that his college application would be accepted should he come to the United States, Zik (as he would soon be called) did what any enterprising boy would do—he stowed away on a freighter bound for America. Unfortunately, the ship was forced to return to port in Ghana, and Azikiwe was stranded. Penniless, he soon found a job there

Nnamdi Azikiwe in traditional Nigerian clothing. His U.S. studies prepared him for a future on the African political stage.

as a police officer. On a visit to Ghana, Azikiwe's mother persuaded him to come home to Nigeria. Upon his return, his father provided funds to travel to the United States.

The temperatures and changing foliage in Harpers Ferry in early October 1925 might have presented a physical shock to Azikiwe—a boy who grew up in the tropics—but his years of being taught in a number of primary, secondary, and parochial schools must have influenced the positive and genial attitude he took toward this scholastic venture in another country. With McDonald's guidance, Zik enrolled in the 1925-26 program, which emphasized a liberal academic course of study. He took courses in botany, zoology, advanced algebra, Latin language and literature, and French language and literature. Completing these courses, he began the 1926-27 year studying astronomy, geology, trigonometry, additional Latin, philosophy, and sociology.

Azikiwe was introduced to American football early at Storer, the result of which he undoubtedly ate more than a few measures of dirt on Camp Hill. He participated in other sports programs as well. His strength was in track and field; however, he also excelled in boxing, swimming, soccer, and tennis.

Finances always presented a challenge in his early years in America. Between academics and sports, Zik held a variety of jobs including dishwasher, coal miner, elevator operator, car washer, kitchen help, and waiter. At Storer he even operated an independent pawn shop and a typing service.

Following graduation in 1927, Zik began advanced studies, first at Howard University in Washington, DC, where he studied with Ralph Bunche, who would go on to become the first African American to receive the Nobel Peace Prize. Due to financial difficulties, Zik left Howard in 1929 and enrolled in Pennsylvania's Lincoln University. There he received a bachelor's degree with honors in political science in 1930 and a master's in religion and philosophy in 1932. His finances improved when he was employed as a teaching assistant at Lincoln. He received a scholarship to study journalism at Columbia University and concurrently pursued a PhD there on the topic of Liberian diplomacy. He began his path into journalism at this time, working as a columnist for the *Baltimore Afro-American* and *Philadelphia Tribune* newspapers and the Associated Negro Press.

In 1933, Zik finished two master's degree programs in anthropology and political science at the University of Pennsylvania and was appointed a full-time lecturer in political science. He also taught ancient, medieval, and modern world history, as well as English and African history. Azikiwe received many honorary degrees from the schools he attended, including an honorary Doctorate of Law from Lincoln University in 1934. A former Lincoln classmate also received that honor—Thurgood Marshall, who became Associate Justice of the Supreme Court of the United States.

Those steps up the U.S. academic ladder strengthened Azikiwe for the next extraordinary period of his life. Zik believed his American education prepared him for three particular professions: teaching, journalism, and diplomacy.

Finally in 1934, after nearly a decade of university studies in the United States, Nnamdi Azikiwe felt it was time to return home to Nigeria. He accepted an offer to edit the *African Morning Post* in Accra, Ghana, and in 1937 he founded the *West African Pilot* in Lagos. Within a decade, Azikiwe was controlling six daily newspapers, all aggressive voices in support of nationalism. His expressive views moved him onto the political stage, where he held a number of public offices over the next twenty years. In 1960, Nigeria finally gained independence from the British Commonwealth. Three years later, on October 1, 1963, Nigeria became a republic, and the Rt. Hon. Dr. Nnamdi Azikiwe was named leader of this young independent country.

A wealth of biographical resources highlight the accomplishments of this remarkable man who had early roots at Storer. In addition to writing poetry and an autobiography, Azikiwe authored over two dozen books or journals largely dedicated to African history and his nationalistic and political views. He was a member of many varied organizations and societies, broadly ranging from the Anti-Slavery Society for the Protection of Human Rights to the British Association for the Advancement of Science, and the American Society of International Law. He actively participated in sports throughout his life and won letters, medals, and trophies at every university or venue that he attended. He belonged to the Amateur Athletic Association of Nigeria, Nigerian Swimming Association, Nigerian Boxing Board of Control, and Nigerian Cricket Association, and he was on the Nigeria Olympic Committee.

Once, during this dynamic life, Nnamdi Azikiwe did return to the little college on the hill overlooking Harpers Ferry. In 1947, as a Doctor of Philosophy and international statesman, he delivered the commencement address to another generation of Storer students. In his address Dr. Azikiwe said, "Courage, brother, do not stumble; though the path be dark as night, there's a star to guide the humble. Trust in God, and do the right."

After a lengthy illness, Dr. Nnamdi Azikiwe died May 11, 1996, at the Nigeria Teaching Hospital. He was ninety-two years old. He is buried in his native home at Onitsha. Places honoring his name in Nigeria include the Nnamdi Azikiwe International Airport in Abuja, the Nnamdi Azikiwe Stadium in Enugu, and the Nnamdi Azikiwe University in Awka. Numerous streets and buildings are named for him, and his portrait is imprinted on Nigeria's five hundred naira currency note.

A skeptic might propose that Azikiwe—with his native intelligence and passion—would have accomplished all that he did even had he not come to Harpers Ferry. Whether by choice or chance, Storer College can be rightfully proud of its role in the drama of this great man.

CHAPTER 21

Fight On, Golden Tornado:
The School Spirit of Storer Athletics

By Creighton Waters

For many students, an important facet of the college experience is participating in or cheering for the school's athletic program. At Storer College, it was no different. Between 1899 and 1955, the "Golden Tornado"—as Storer's mascot was called—fielded teams in no less than five sports. The camaraderie, sportsmanship, exercise, and character-building of Storer's teams benefitted countless student athletes, and were integral parts of the school's pride and culture. While Storer athletics never attained the fame or financial clout associated with modern Division I college sports, they did provide other invaluable rewards to students, shaping them as strong, confident young men and women against the harsh world of segregation that awaited them outside the campus.

Early Storer teams tended to compete against African American high schools in the Washington/Baltimore area, such as Armstrong and M Street (later known as Dunbar) Schools. Storer also played predominantly African American colleges, including Howard University, Morgan State University, and Bluefield Institute (Bluefield State), as well as a variety of "athletic clubs" in towns throughout the region. When the Middle Atlantic Athletic Association was formed in 1931, Storer's opponents expanded to include Cheyney State and Downingtown Industrial of Pennsylvania, Bordentown Industrial of New Jersey, Bowie State and Princess Anne Academy (now the University of Maryland-Eastern Shore) from Maryland, and Delaware State.

Storer College athletics began in 1899 with the creation of a football team. Baseball and track and field arrived in 1907, while the 1920s saw the addition of basketball for both men and women. Boxing was also practiced sporadically throughout the school's history. But football would always remain the most well-known, popular sport at Storer. The football team was even given its own colors—gold and white—rather than the standard "Crimson and Old Gold" worn by other Storer teams.

Over its fifty-six year tenure, the Golden Tornado football team compiled a record of sixty wins, seventy losses, and thirteen tied games. An April 1916 article in the *Storer Record* sung praises of the "mighty Storer Football Team" that had finished the 1915 season with three wins, zero losses, and one tie. The student journalist claimed he was "very upset" because an unnamed sports magazine had dared announce M Street High School in Washington, DC, as the "champion football team of the secondary schools of the Middle South," when the author believed "Storer had a much better team." The 1921 team was arguably the greatest in the school's history, finishing with five wins, one loss, and zero ties, including a 124-0 drubbing of the Hagerstown (Maryland) Athletic Club. Regarding some of the later teams, Mary Harris, Class of 1950,

Football practice on the sloping lawn in front of Anthony Memorial Hall, 1909. Early teams competed against African American high schools in the Baltimore–Washington area.

recalled, "We didn't win very often, but when we did, you would have thought we had just won the Super Bowl!"

In the beginning, the football team usually practiced and hosted games on Storer's campus. But after the new Harpers Ferry High School was constructed in 1930, Storer frequently played on that more spacious field. A 1950s' player once commented that he "hated home games." When pressed on this, he remarked that the coach "made us run about a half mile up the hill on Washington Street in cleats and full pads to the high school field to greet our opponents. We would be out of breath when we arrived and the visiting team would step off their bus looking refreshed and ready for business!"

Right end Russell Roper remembered playing against Cheyney State of Chester County, Pennsylvania, in 1947. "We beat Cheyney seven to nothing, and I caught the winning pass," Roper said proudly in a recent interview. Roper, a 1950 graduate, noted that there was much camaraderie on the football team and that all the players were good students and young men of the "finest moral character."

Storer's annual homecoming football game was traditionally held on the first Saturday in November and was a major social event for the student body. In his senior year, 1953 graduate William Vollin was the team's captain; his future wife, Anna, was homecoming queen (also sometimes known as "Miss Tornado"). In 2009, on the eve

Homecoming queen and her court at football game, ca. 1950s. The quarterback traditionally handed the game ball to the queen, also call "Miss Tornado."

of their fifty-sixth wedding anniversary, Anna recalled that William "presented the game ball to me at half-time of our homecoming game." After graduation, both William and Anna served long, noteworthy careers in public education, and their three children all went on to earn college degrees.

The games often received coverage in local newspapers, which provided highlights of the football team through the years.

> Storer College and Armstrong Tech [High School] played a stubborn, scoreless football game at Union League Park Saturday afternoon. The game was replete with thrills. Tech, through three periods, put up a strong offensive and defensive game, twice getting the ball within 5 yards of Storer's goal, but the mountain lads held like adamant, and Tech was baffled.—*Washington Herald*, November 21, 1910.

> M Street Academy [High School] lost to Storer by 21 to 0.... Storer College of Harpers Ferry showed striking improvement. Each year Storer, a small college, is creeping nearer collegiate standing athletically.—*Washington Herald*, December 4, 1910

In a rare Thursday afternoon contest on November 26, 1914, in Pittsburgh, Pennsylvania, Storer fought the home team Delaney Rifles Athletic Club:

Wylie Avenue produced too much weight and speed yesterday for the Storer College football team and the Delaney Rifles won a victory, 32 to 0…. The lads from Harpers Ferry were never able to cope with the whirlwinds from the hill district, nor were they able to make any impression on the powerful line they had to face. —*Pittsburgh Post-Gazette*, November 27, 1914

Fully 500 lovers of football attended the Delaney Rifle – Storer College game at Tech stadium Thursday afternoon and both teams had partisans galore present, decked out in either the blue and white of the Delaneys, or the yellow and white of the Storer contingent. Both sides were confident of victory and between the uproar of the First brigade K. of P. band, which streaked the atmosphere with ragtime selections every few minutes, and the yells, catcalls, and noise disturbers of the rooters for the two teams, about the only quiet moments were between quarters…. In the last quarter one of the Storer boys, Payne, the fullback, got the ball on a fumble, on their 35 yard line and skirting the Delaney's right end went down the field for 65 yards with both teams trailing behind him. He looked good to make a touchdown, but after a spectacular run by Campbell was downed on the Delaney 10 yard line. That was the only time the visiting team looked at all dangerous. —*Pittsburgh Press*, November 29, 1914

A sportswriter gave this spirited report on a game November 22, 1927:

Flashing a ripping, tearing, smashing defense that would not be denied, Bluefield Institute's Big Blue eleven swamped a sturdy, hard-fighting crew from Storer College, at Harper's Ferry, winning a well-deserved 49–0 count after sixty minutes of real football, at the Institute bowl yesterday afternoon…. The real strength of Storer is not indicated by the score, for the visiting crew put up a defense that had the Bluefield eleven at a dead stand-still at times, forcing Drew of Bluefield to send the pigskin down the field from his reliable toe. It was Graves, Cain and Wiggins aided by a perfectly performing line, who turned Storer's highest hopes into the depths of despair, as time and again the Blue ball carrying aces slipped through nicely, opened holes in the line, turned, twisted, side-stepped, and dodged their way for 10, 15, 20, and 25-yard gains, sometimes carrying two and three would-be tacklers for five or six yards before being fully stopped." —*Pittsburgh Courier*, November 26, 1927

Baseball

In contrast to the football team's fame, baseball was unfortunately the least doc-umented of all the school's sports teams. However, in the *Storer College Sentinel*, 1909-1910—just a couple years after baseball was initiated at Storer—Athletic Editor G. Frank Taylor wrote about the second game of the season:

> At the beginning of the game everyone was on nettles, because the score was one nothing in favor of Purcellville up to the fifth inning. At the beginning of the sixth inning Storer rallied as usual. Every man at the bat got a clean hit. Some made a two bagger and others made home runs. At the beginning of the eighth inning you could hear the calls over in the bleachers for the fire department to put Storer out. The score was 17 to 1 in favor of Storer.

Track and Field

Records show that in 1907, the same year Storer established its baseball team, the athletic department further expanded to include track and field. In its first season, the Storer team traveled to Washington, DC, to compete in a track meet against three other predominantly African American schools: Howard University, M Street High School, and Armstrong Manual Training School. Washington's *Evening Star* newspaper

President McDonald with the Storer College baseball team in 1911.

Track and Field team of 1921. Note the trophy and Storer pennant in the foreground.

reported "a large audience" turned out to watch the event. Storer athletes placed first in the 100 yard dash, 220 yard dash, and standing broad jump, and scored second in the pole vault. However, these successes did not provide enough points to make Storer the overall winner of the meet: "Storer was runner up to M Street by a score of 75-44," said the *Star*. "The Storer students were the guests of the M Street students, and were entertained at a reception at True Reformers' Hall Saturday evening. President Henry T. McDonald of Storer College expressed himself as well pleased with every feature of the trip, except for the number of events his boys had been able to win."

The class of 1925 brought the track and field team one of its brightest stars: Nnamdi "Zik" Azikiwe of Nigeria. Azikiwe proved to be an extremely talented all-around athlete, excelling in the high jump and cross country running. Azikiwe also participated in boxing, representing Storer against all challengers as the defending regional welterweight champion for two years. Also an excellent swimmer and soccer player, Azikiwe went on to become the first democratically-elected president of Nigeria in 1963.

News of Storer track and field successes even reached as far as Pittsburgh, Pennsylvania. On May 3, 1941, the *Pittsburgh Courier* described a meet held at Howard University. Although Howard won the most points in the match overall, the *Courier* noted that "Storer College's Theodore Munro sprinted down the cinderpath to victory in both the 100 and 220 yard dashes," and that another Storer student, M. Wilson, "captured the high-jump with a leap of 5 feet 6 inches."

Basketball

Basketball came to Storer in the 1920s—for men *and* women. Cagers—as basketball players were sometimes called—played their home games in the Robinson Barn on campus, which was converted into the school's gymnasium in 1921. However, Storer's financial challenges sometimes impacted the athletes. Elbert Norton, Class of 1955, played basketball and a number of other sports, as well as singing in the college choir. In an oral history interview, he said he was "strongly encouraged" by then-president Leonard Terrell to skip a basketball game road trip and attend a fundraising concert. Storer was in danger of being closed due to a failing budget, and the choral groups, traveling to black and white churches throughout the region, had become an integral source of badly-need donations. "They were trying to do everything they could to save Storer," Norton said.

The men's team generated much excitement over the years, and this was reflected in local newspapers:

> In one of the most interesting basketball games played this season Storer College defeated Miner T.C. [Teachers College], 50 to 18. Beginning with a fast pace that at times became almost dizzy, Storer launched an attack that bewildered the T.C. cagers. The Storer machine started clicking away early in the game and kept the lead until the final whistle blew. —*Pittsburgh Courier,* April 2, 1932

> The Hagerstown Zephyrs basketball team trimmed Storer College Varsity of Harpers Ferry by final score of 28-27, on the Armory floor here last night before a capacity crowd. The game furnished plenty of thrills with Storer out front in the third quarter. The Zephyrs put on the pressure and forged to the front in the final quarter to win. —*Daily Mail* (Hagerstown, Maryland), February 16, 1940

> The Crispus Attucks Mighty Mites cagers (York, Pennsylvania) lost an interesting contest last evening on the Smallwood floor to the Storer College five, 27 to 25…. Myers' foul gave the local team the lead but Parks caged a foul goal and followed that with a field goal to give the College team the victory. Parks finished the game with eleven points. —*Gazette and Daily* (York), March 7, 1941

It was the women's team, however, which was arguably the most successful of all Storer sports teams. Best friends Doris Gaiters and Genevieve Bradford, both 1941 graduates of Storer College, starred on the women's basketball team during their

Basketball games were played in the Robinson Barn on campus, which was converted to a gymnasium in 1921. Substandard athletic facilities were always an issue and "home" games were often played at nearby public schools and rented fields.

school careers. In an oral history interview, Doris joked that she played the position of center for the team because "I was the tallest girl!" Genevieve also pointed out proudly in an interview that "one night I scored forty points for our team in that old barn!" Newspapers recorded highlights of the team's play:

> The Storer College Girls' Basketball team, led by pretty Ethel Roades, defeated the Hartshorn Memorial College team of Richmond, Va. 16 – 12 in a fast, interesting game. —*Pittsburgh Courier*, February 27, 1926

> The Storer College Girls' basketball team from Harpers Ferry, W. Va., will oppose the Forster Street 'Y' Girls' team (Harrisburg, Pennsylvania) on the YMCA floor this Friday evening at 8:30 o'clock. The college girls defeated the 'Y' girls by a score of 32 – 27 at Harper's Ferry about two weeks ago and the 'Y' girls are practicing hard to avenge the defeat. —*Harrisburg Telegraph*, February 6, 1941

The ladies' basketball team was also frequently lauded in the press for their sportsmanship:

Women's basketball champions of the MAAA league in 1940. Miss Doris Gaiters is in the center with her best friend Miss Genevieve Bradford on the right. The female athletes were often praised for their sportsmanship. (Photo courtesy of Doris Gaiters)

Carver High School (Cumberland, Maryland) girls also lost in the finals last night (in the "Tri-State Athletic Union Tournament") going down before the Storer College girls, 18 to 8 in a snappy game of ball…. Trophies, plaques, and medals were awarded to teams and individual players. Plaques were presented to Storer, Carver, and Leesburg girls in that order. Best sportsmanship award—a plaque, was presented to the girls of the Storer College team…. Award for best sportsmanship for girls went to Miss Handy of Storer, a cash award given by Referee "Spike" Herboldsheimer—*Cumberland Evening Times*, March 31, 1945

Storer's student athletes found success in a variety of career fields after they left the school's hallowed halls. Lessons learned in competitions on hardwood floors and grassy green fields helped them become positive members of a society that didn't always treat them fairly. Football player Russell Roper, Class of 1950, summarized the heart of Storer College athletics succinctly in a recent interview. Recalling his physical education teacher, Wallace Darius, Roper said that Darius, like the entire Storer faculty, cared deeply for the students and wanted to see them succeed in society after graduation. "So lessons learned went beyond winning on the football field but also winning in all walks of life."

1920 Storer College football team.

Every August the living alumni and their families return to the former Storer College campus among the West Virginia hills for their annual school reunion and share heartfelt memories of carrying the banner for the Crimson and Old Gold. The spirit of Storer College athletics will always live on thanks to this special group of people who wore the jersey of the "Golden Tornado."

OFFICIAL COLLEGE YELL (1909)
Storer College Sentinel 1909 - 1910

Rah! Rah! Rah!
Rah! Rah! Rah!
Rah! Rah! Rah!
Storer! Storer! Storer!
S-t-o-r-e-r.

CHAPTER 22

"Those Things of the Past"
The Storer Community and the "Faithful Slave" Monument

By John M. Rudy

There was a modest crowd gathered along Potomac Street in Harpers Ferry that October day in 1931. Many were locals, "Confederate Daughters and veterans and sympathizers," the *Washington Post* noted. Some came from West Virginia. Others hailed from nearby Maryland or Virginia. At least one face in that crowd, however, was from decidedly farther north, and tinged just a shade or two darker than those of the white veterans of the rebel army and their daughters. Several decades before, her parents had lived in a nation where, had they wandered into Harpers Ferry from their home in New England on a bad day, they might have been mistakenly sold as human property. Now, amid a sea of Confederate sympathizers, Pearl Tatten stood and spoke truth to the gathered crowd.

"I am the daughter of a Connecticut volunteer, who wore the blue, who fought for the freedom of my people." Tatten addressed the white audience clearly, bravely, and unbidden. Women and men across the American South had been lynched for doing less. Behind her, the college choir she led each week, young black men and women striving for a place in American society, stood ready to sing. But she kept speaking. "Today we are looking forward to the future," she scolded the crowd intent on grasping tightly to the racial dichotomy of the Confederacy, "forgetting those things of the past."

Pearl Tatten, a slight woman about five feet tall and weighing all of 100 pounds, then turned on her heels and struck up the choir while the audience sat stunned. "It was like a bolt from the blue," a newspaper reporter wrote later, "and it struck home." The choir sang a hymn of supplication—a reminder to the audience of what humility meant. It was a negro spiritual: "Tis Me, Oh Lord, Standing in the Need of Prayer."

Confederate veterans groups had been discussing a monument for Harpers Ferry for almost thirty years before Pearl Tatten spoke up at its eventual dedication. In May of 1922, the Harpers Ferry Town Council received a formal request, addressed to and forwarded on from the Baltimore & Ohio Railroad, from "General" Julian S. Carr, Commander-in-Chief of the United Confederate Veterans. "I have been approached," Carr informed the town's mayor and council, "by the Daughters of the Confederacy and the Sons of Confederate Veterans to beg of you that they be allowed to place a boulder now in their possession in the triangle at Harper's Ferry." The boulder was to "commemorate the memory of the faithful slave, Haywood Shepherd [sic], a negro who was the first victim of the John Brown Raid on Harper's Ferry." Heyward Shepherd *was* indeed the first victim of John Brown's raid on the town, but Carr's assertion that he was a "faithful slave" was erroneous. In October 1859, Shepherd was a free

A crowd gathers on Potomac Street on October 10, 1931, for the dedication of the Heyward Shepherd monument. As Storer President Henry McDonald addresses the crowd, some of the Storer College choir members can be seen just to the left of the telephone pole next to the stage. Though difficult to see, the girls are dressed in white shirts with a dark, loosely knotted tie and the boys are in suits. The white obelisk in the background (right) marks the original location of the John Brown Fort.

black employed by the railroad, and likely did not even know the motives of Brown's raiders when he was killed.

One member of the town council had a larger stake in the outcome of the request. Henry T. McDonald served as council recorder—the town's corresponding secretary—but he was also president of Storer College, the local scion of African American education. When the letter arrived from General Carr, McDonald set to work at once. "We went over the question of the wisdom of allowing the Sons of Confederate Veterans and the Daughters of the Confederacy to erect a monument to Heyward Shepherd," the president recorded in his family historical files, making sure to spell the victim of John Brown's raid correctly where the general did not. At the May 30th town council meeting, McDonald lobbied hard. "Last night at the Council meeting," he wrote the following day, "I saw to it that the offer was rejected." The bid for a monument was dead.

McDonald, on behalf of the town council, wrote to the B&O Railroad's president with the news. "After mature deliberation I have to report to you that it was the unanimous vote that we gratefully acknowledge the desire…to perpetuate the memory of faithful slaves." Still, the monument had no place in Harpers Ferry. "We look with disfavor upon the placing in our midst such a monument as proposed," McDonald continued, "as being likely to occasion unpleasant racial feeling." The conclusion was clear to the town council. "We see no good purpose that can be served in this case and believe that harm would result to our community."

Less than a decade later, with a new mayor sympathetic to the South, and a slightly revised request, the boulder came anyway. "A monument to 'true' slaves will be unveiled," the *Baltimore Afro-American* editorialized on October 3, 1931. Quoting a press release from the United Daughters of the Confederacy, the *Afro* indignantly parroted the southern daughters' words. "The project to erect a monument in memory of the slaves who remained faithful during the raid has been planned by the UDC for many years." The newspaper's editors turned to W. E. B. Du Bois' biography of John Brown, quoting from it like sacred scripture of the struggle for freedom. "The account of John Brown's battle with Federal troops at Harpers Ferry" was peppered with slaves rising to fight. The editors included a potent quote of how Brown's raiders "met several colored men; they immediately agreed to join us. They said they had long been waiting." That the monument was rising in Harpers Ferry to loyal slaves, the *Afro* blithely noted, was fine. But, "it is important for us to note," the paper concluded that "slaves or descendants of slaves fell at Harpers Ferry and that in the hearts of thousands more the spark of freedom flamed."

One of the *Baltimore Afro-American*'s readers was Storer College's choir director, Pearl Tatten. Although her choir had been asked to sing for the dedication, she had not quite understood its aims until reading the stinging critiques in the *Afro*. The front page of the newspaper a week later noted not only the UDC's motivation, but Storer College's open cooperation in the dedication. The shock that a Baltimore black minister was taking part in the affair "was only increased when the printed program showed that Henry T. McDonald, white, president of Storer College, at Harpers Ferry (a colored institution) will also take part in the 'Uncle Tom' celebration." The paper's editors quoted liberally from a letter President McDonald had written to them a few days before. "I may say that those in charge invited me to give a short address of welcome," he told the paper, adding that, "the college glee club will sing a number of sacred songs." The dedication, McDonald was sure, could "voice the spirit of fellowship and enduring good will. It is a fine expression of a new era of inter-racial understanding."

After reading in the *Baltimore Afro-American* exactly what the event held in store, the choir director took a sheet of college letterhead and a pen in hand. She neatly crossed out President McDonald's name from the page—this letter was coming from her desk, not his—and wrote:

After reading this article, I wonder if we should have a part in the exercises. When I talked with you I did not see the attitude of the U.D.C. Do you think we should appear on such a program when we honor John Brown and feel that while he may have used the wrong methods, his motive was just? I feel now that should we take part we would be most inconsistent.

Tatten paper clipped the newspaper article to the letter and delivered it to President McDonald.

On October 10, 1931, Elizabeth Burford Bashinsky, UDC President, stood at the podium along Potomac Street, perched atop the embankment of the Baltimore & Ohio Railroad. The Alabamian greeted her crowd and the distinguished guests: "Members and chairman of the Faithful Slave Memorial Committee." The dedication was already becoming exactly what Pearl Tatten had feared. President Mc-Donald's tepid remarks did little to distance Storer College from the monument. And now the president of the UDC was laying bare exactly why the group was there with no pretense.

As Bashinsky spoke, the inconsistency became abundantly clear to anyone paying even the slightest attention. "We are asked sometimes," the Confederate apologist mused, "'Why look backwards?'" But the UDC held it was not looking backwards. "Looking backwards is looking forward; those who do not look backward never look forward." Bashinsky's backwards gaze was wistful, even longing. Born two years after the

Pearl Tatten (second row from back, center) and the Storer College choir.

war had ended, two years after slavery had been wiped unceremoniously from the nation, the Alabama daughter had no real concept of what slavery had been. That, however, did not stop her from commenting on its utility. "People unfamiliar with the patriarchal relationship between the whites of the South and the Negro do not understand the conditions. For logical reasons the people of the South inherited slavery, but with all the responsibilities that…a Christian conscience could impose." Slavery was a righteous system to Bashinsky—it bettered the black race.

But Bashinsky's understanding of the perspective of African Americans was gauze thin. Standing with a black choir behind her, she proudly proclaimed to the audience: "The black mammy. Oh! The black mammy," she reminisced, "how she loved her white 'chillun.'" Bashinsky's own "mammy never left me until I married." That perceived loyalty of black to white impressed her. "How could anyone get these sons of these black mammies to take up arms against their masters?"

Behind her, Pearl Tatten had already had enough. She rose with her choir after the Daughters placed a wreath beside the new monument. Someone announced that the choir would now sing. "In the few moments that followed a voice calm, penetrating and cutting, smote the air," the *Afro* reported. As she spoke, Pearl Tatten "cut out the vitals of every speech that had been made." Using the UDC president's own words against her, Pearl Tatten quickly and decisively excoriated the argument of racial inequity in a "release of a pent-up fire that had to find expression, of a deep-seated sympathy for John Brown and for the views of modern youth."

I am the daughter of a Connecticut volunteer, who wore the blue, who fought for the freedom of my people, for which John Brown struck the first blow. Today we are looking forward to the future, forgetting those things of the past. We are pushing forward to a larger freedom, not in the spirit of the black mammy but in the spirit of new freedom and rising youth.

Private Charles S. Tatten had joined the 29th Connecticut Infantry—a segregated unit akin to the 54th and 55th Massachusetts—on December 2, 1863, at New Haven, exactly four years after John Brown's execution. Born in Buffalo, New York, Tatten had likely come east in his job as a railroad porter. Tatten had been decently educated before the war began; he knew how to read and write. As a soldier, Tatten had worked his way up through the ranks. By the time the Confederate capital at Richmond, Virginia, fell, he was 1st Sergeant Charles Tatten. The 29th Connecticut Infantry was the first regiment to march into the city, liberating the black population and driving one of the final nails into slavery's coffin.

Pearl Tatten was a daughter of a veteran of the War of the Rebellion just as Bashinsky was. Growing up in the 1880s and 1890s, Pearl had learned what the blue uniform meant to men and women with black skin. But the UDC members in the audience had an entirely different opinion. After her choir finished piping Negro spirituals into the decidedly white event, a note was handed up to the stage. Pearl unfolded it and read the hastily scribbled words. "I wonder at your temerity. Your untimely remarks were out of place, in poor spirit and most discourteous."

But Pearl Tatten was undeterred. "I certainly do not wish to create bitterness," she told a reporter, "but I could not stand there and hear those things without being deeply hurt." She knew what was in her heart and she could guess what was in the heart of each of her black students hearing the hateful invective of the day. "I just had to speak out and say what was crying to be said." But there was a smirk to that defiance. When faced with the note, Tatten could easily deny it had any effect. She told the reporter, "I merely consider the source of its contents."

"It is regrettable that a monument 'honoring' (?) slaves who were faithful to the Confederacy, should have been erected and dedicated in Harpers Ferry, West Virginia," Charles E. Hill, Storer class of 1900, wrote to the *Baltimore Afro-American* a few weeks after the dedication. After all, Harpers Ferry was where "the John Brown raid struck the first physical blow for the abolition of slavery—that accursed institution, which exacted 250 years' labor from our race." But the worse regret, the Storer College alumnus wrote, was that his alma mater had anything to do with the dedication. The new monument "is not an inspiration to colored students—it being rather a symbol of that inferiority complex which the slaves could not evade; but this complex has no place in modern education."

But President McDonald, Hill wrote, "endorses such a program by making the welcome address, and by insisting that the students sing, he is creating an attitude of servility in the

"Faithful Slave" monument today in Lower Town Harpers Ferry. (NPS photo)

students' minds." It was clear to Hill that an event glorifying "the 'Uncle Toms' and 'Black Mammies' has no place in any plan of colored advancement, and thoughtful progressive colored folk resent to the utmost every attempt to humiliate and subjugate (in spirit) the race."

McDonald was compelled to respond, at least in private. He patiently but sternly explained that "it is a monument to <u>a freeman</u> who exemplified the 'character and faithfulness' of other men and women." Any nuance and depth of the oppression felt by Hill was obviously lost on McDonald. Copying the text of the monument, the president asserted that the faithfulness and loyalty outweighed any seeming inferiority that the monument might convey.

Then, as to Hill's contention that the students were forced to participate, McDonald took offense. "You suggest that the President of Storer insisted upon the students singing and thus undermining their high ideals. Nothing could be more remote from the facts." Seemingly forgetting any protest Pearl Tatten had brought before the fact, McDonald held that "the glee club was invited to sing," and that they had "cheerfully assented" to do so. Above all, however, McDonald just wanted the issue to go away. At the bottom of his reply, he wrote a short note: "This letter, of course, is not for publication. It is better to let the affair now rest."

Hill wrote back, indignant at the paternalistic and patronizing tone of President McDonald's letter. "I am not," he said, quoting the president's accusation, "unhappily misinformed." In fact, Hill could seemingly see the truth that McDonald failed to see. The Confederate heritage groups simply "used Heywood [sic] Shepherd and his admirable qualities as a camaflage [sic] to cloak their real motives, which are to counteract the memory and influence of John Brown's raid and also to place a premium on 'Uncle Toms and Black Mammies.'" Hill, who lived in the largely segregated city of Washington, DC, knew full well what the UDC wanted. They certainly did not "stand for the broadest progress and advancement of colored people, and this fact is evidenced in the southern states by 'Jim Crow' cars, denial of the right to vote, segregation, lynchings, peonage and limited public school facilities."

The course of action Charles Hill would have rather seen from his alma mater was clear. "If the invitation had been politely declined," he wrote McDonald, "it would have made many new friends for Storer College, especially in our group." But now, with the bad press and the seeming embrace of Confederate heritage, "the exact opposite is true, because we, as a race, will not take this latest 'slap in the face' lying down."

"The Birthday Basket"
The Gifts and Talents of Dr. Richard I. McKinney

By Creighton Waters

I n the spring of 2004, middle school students from Jefferson County, West Virginia, came to Harpers Ferry National Historical Park to learn about Storer College's legacy as one of the first desegregated institutions of higher learning in American history. In the Curtis Freewill Baptist Church on the college's former campus, the eighth graders sat with rapt attention as a ninety-seven-year-old speaker's wisdom echoed off the walls of the church:

> You came into this world with a "Birthday Basket." We all have a "Birthday Basket." What is in that basket? You were born with certain abilities that are peculiar to you. It may be the ability to play a musical instrument or to master a language quicker than somebody else. Your ongoing education will help bring those positive qualities out. They're there…it's just a matter of what you do with them. Storer College was designed to be a place where young people could get all of those talents within them brought out to help them advance into a bright and hopeful world.

The college president, Dr. Richard I. McKinney, attends a tea with a group of coeds. One of the advantages of attending a small college was getting to know faculty and staff.

Chapter 23 ❧ Page 143

President McKinney (center) on the Storer College campus, ca. 1944. McKinney was the school's first African American president and first to hold an academic doctoral degree.

The students leaned forward with anticipation, awaiting the next words of Dr. Richard Ishmael McKinney, a living testimony to the perseverance of Storer College.

Richard McKinney was born August 8, 1906, in Live Oak, Florida, on the college campus of Farmer Institute (later named Florida Memorial College). He was the youngest of nine children whose father was a Baptist minister and educator. His father's deep faith and insistence on a strong education rubbed off on McKinney and guided him the rest of his life. McKinney's mother told him at a young age, "Richard, you can do anything you set your mind to."

Despite growing up in the South in a world of racial segregation and inequality, McKinney said later of his mother's words, "I believed it. And acted on it." McKinney often credited the "rags to riches" young adult novels of nineteenth-century writer Horatio Alger as giving him hope that he could overcome any challenges that faced him in a cruel society. His parents were so committed to giving their children a quality education that they sent them all away to schools that provided better opportunities than could be found at home.

McKinney graduated as valedictorian of his high school class at Morehouse Academy in Atlanta, Georgia, in 1927. In 1931, McKinney received his AB degree in religion and philosophy from Morehouse College. He continued graduate study in religion and philosophy at Pendle Hill, a Quaker school in Wallingford, Pennsylvania.

After a year at Pendle Hill, McKinney transferred to the Andover Newton Theological School in Newton, Massachusetts. While attending Andover, McKinney began his ministry, preaching at the Pond Street Baptist Church in Providence, Rhode Island. McKinney completed his bachelor of divinity degree at Andover in 1934 with a thesis entitled, "The Problem of Evil and its Relation to the Ministry to an Under-privileged Minority." In 1937, he also earned a masters of sacred theology degree from Andover.

Friends tried to discourage McKinney from pursuing a doctorate, worried that he would meet rejection. Despite these warnings, he enrolled at Yale University and earned a PhD in the philosophy of higher education in 1942, with a dissertation on "Religion in Higher Education among Negroes." In a 1996 interview with the *Baltimore Sun*, Dr. McKinney said, "Although I didn't know anybody with a PhD in philosophy, I always expected to go to the top of academe. When I mentioned it to one of my professors, he said, 'You don't need a doctorate.' Of course, I paid no attention to him…. After I got mine, he eventually got his."

After Yale, McKinney conducted post-doctoral work at the University of Chicago, Columbia University, and at the Sorbonne in Paris, France. McKinney's first academic appointment was at Virginia Union University in Richmond, Virginia, where he was

A large gathering of students and faculty with President McKinney (front row, center) on October 13, 1945. This photo was taken one month after the end of WWII. The future looked bright with an expected upsurge in enrollment by returning veterans on the G.I. bill.

Assistant Professor of Philosophy and Religion and Director of Religious Activities. He later assumed the post of Dean of the School of Religion.

In 1944, at the age of thirty-eight, McKinney accepted an offer to become president of Storer College. McKinney's hire was significant—he was the first African American president in the history of the school. McKinney was also the first president in the history of the school to hold an academic doctoral degree. The legacy of Storer—one of the first desegregated schools in post-slavery America—certainly made McKinney's hiring as president a watershed moment for the historic college.

McKinney's tenure at Storer College faced many difficulties. Discrimination and local segregation challenged him upon arrival. McKinney came to Harpers Ferry with his wife Phyllis and two young children. During their first night in the president's home on campus, McKinney awoke to find a burning cross on his front lawn. Commenting on this later in life he said, "The community wasn't too happy with my being there. They were never happy with the school to begin with. My children laughed at [the burning cross], and I didn't take it too seriously. I went about my work."

McKinney witnessed firsthand how discrimination affected his predominately black student body. One particular incident almost cost the life of an African American student on the campus. McKinney related this story in an interview:

> There was a tennis court in front of the boys' dormitory. One day one of my top students was there playing tennis and the ball went over an iron picket fence. The student tried to jump over the fence to retrieve the ball and missed. He fell onto one of the pickets and pierced his stomach. We placed him in a car and took him to Charles Town to the nearest hospital where they refused to wait on him because of his color. There was a Catholic hospital [Kings Daughters] in Martinsburg and we took him there. They took him in and nurtured him to health. One couldn't feel safe if you couldn't get medical attention in an emergency. If it hadn't been for that other hospital this young man could have died.

In addition to local opposition and blatant racism, McKinney faced a myriad of other challenges as soon as he set foot on the Storer College campus. McKinney's predecessor, Henry Temple McDonald, served from 1899 to 1944, and after forty-five years of authority was asked to resign by the school's Board of Trustees. When McKinney took over, McDonald didn't assist with the transfer of power, and in fact spoke out publicly against the new president. Dr. McKinney inherited a financially unstable institution with a growing budget deficit. While an impatient board awaited a quick turnaround, McKinney travelled away from the campus for days at a time in an attempt to fundraise with various institutions and trusts.

McKinney's philosophy for Storer College was to give his students a quality education in a Christian environment and every advantage possible in a society that provided them very little opportunity. The "separate but equal" policies of segregation were evident as soon as students walked off the oasis of the school campus. McKinney once said, "Storer College was a place where the young black men and women in a segregated society could get an education…. This school stands for emphasis upon giving light and learning through young minds."

In later years McKinney also spoke about how it was common practice at the time for the student body to stand up when a college president entered the room. "I felt the students didn't need to do that for me. I wanted to have them feel closer to me than having me way up on some pedestal where they had to stand up and acknowledge me. This was an attempt to establish some kind of rapport with them." McKinney and his family also made it a point to attend public and social events that students hosted on campus to strengthen this bond.

Dr. McKinney with Benjamin Nnamdi Azikiwe at the 1947 Storer College commencement.

In 1949, McKinney and his faculty published a series of objectives to address the whole student—intellectually, physically, spiritually, and socially. He established a local chapter of the NAACP on campus and formed a Student Government Association to encourage students to work with faculty to shape the future direction of the school. McKinney also labored to make Storer College a strong four-year institution. He oversaw the construction of a science building and worked to have the State of West Virginia accredit Storer's BA in Elementary Education, as well as the English, home economics, science, and social science sections of its secondary education division.

McKinney's attempts to get full accreditation for the school failed, preventing endowment funds from boosting the annual budget. With his focus always on his students, he fought to establish more pre-med, pre-law, and engineering facilities at the school. The trustees, however, did not support McKinney's ideas for innovation or branching out from traditional curriculum. Years later McKinney stated, "When I saw that we couldn't get the money for building up the school because we were not accredited, I urged the Board of Trustees to abandon the idea of a four-year college competing with other institutions that were accredited, and instead establish a first-class preparatory school." McKinney saw an opportunity to reinvent Storer by creating a first class high school, which would attract students from cities like Washington, DC, Baltimore, and Philadelphia. This attempt to alter Storer's mission was unanimously rejected by the Board of Trustees. The board actually went so far as to take advice on such matters from former president McDonald instead of McKinney.

Caught in the middle of the board's politics, McKinney's position grew tenuous. He had completed several successful ventures at the school regarding facilities and student relations but felt he had accomplished all he could. After commencement exercises in the spring of 1950, McKinney resigned. He later reflected, "I do know that the night on which I tendered my resignation I had the soundest sleep I had in a long time! And I have to add I think that there were about two or three members of the Board who were not unhappy that I resigned." However, he "received a whole sheaf of letters from various people in the community, the editors of newspapers and so on, congratulating me on what I had done."

McKinney spent a brief time at Virginia State College in Petersburg, Virginia, before accepting a position at Morgan State University in Baltimore, Maryland. While a professor at Morgan State, McKinney founded and chaired the Department of Philosophy. McKinney also chaired the Division of Humanities and ultimately served as acting Dean of the College of Arts and Sciences. Officially retiring from Morgan State in 1978, McKinney continued to stay active. He briefly assumed another administrative post as acting Vice President for Academic Affairs at Virginia Union, then returned to Morgan State, where he taught philosophy part-time well into his nineties. McKinney also continued researching, writing, and lecturing independently. He authored several works, including *Mordecai, the Man and His Message*, a 1998 biography of Howard University President Mordecai Wyatt Johnson. In retirement McKinney was also a board member of the Enoch Pratt Free Library and the Reginald E. Lewis Museum of African American History and Culture, and Chairman of the Board of the Union Baptist Church, all located in Baltimore.

On October 28, 2005, McKinney had just given a stirring speech at a conference in Norfolk, Virginia, when he felt tired, asked to lie down, and passed away suddenly. He was 99 years old. Of all Dr. McKinney's accomplishments, the National Park Service is most grateful for the gracious donation of his time to Harpers Ferry National Historical Park. McKinney frequently came back to Harpers Ferry to speak publicly about his time as Storer College president. Well-versed in the history of Storer, McKinney shared his immense knowledge with the public during the park's special events and symposiums.

One of McKinney's last visits to the park included his speech to the group of middle school students about their "Birthday Baskets" and the importance of a sound education. After receiving enthusiastic applause, McKinney quipped, "I like to be around young people, and seeing me they learn that age is just a number." Dr. McKinney's "Birthday Basket" was certainly overflowing with gifts and talents beyond measure. His counsel, institutional knowledge, kindness, and generosity are missed by anyone who had the pleasure of meeting this amazing pioneer in the field of education.

CHAPTER 24

A Gentle Leader Presides at the End:
Reverend Leonard E. Terrell

By James Koenig

The closing of Storer College in 1955 did not surprise anyone familiar with its plight. Founded by Freewill Baptists in 1867 with the goal of providing higher education to former slaves and anyone willing to learn, the college faced daunting challenges from the start. For nearly ninety years, Storer provided schooling for a disadvantaged population that had few options for attaining higher education.

When Reverend Leonard Terrell arrived in May of 1952, the demise of Storer had been in the making for many years. Low student enrollment, inadequate funding, staff turnovers, an aging physical plant, and a balky governing board, in addition to poorly outfitted classrooms and labs, had always been issues that progressively worsened. Outside forces, too, impacted the school: two world wars that depleted the rolls of college-age African American men; the Great Depression that lasted over a decade making employment rather than education a priority for African Americans; and the creation of state-operated schools in direct competition to Storer. By 1952, the college was on institutional life support and surely Rev. Terrell had no illusions about the chances of saving the patient. But he was game to try.

Admittedly, he was not the first or second choice of Storer's Board of Trustees

Reverend Leonard E. Terrell (center) served as college president for the last two years of its existence.

to lead the college. A local newspaper reported that Terrell was "A Baptist minister whose inclinations are more churchy than educational." However, with formidable challenges at every turn, Storer was lucky to find someone with Rev. Terrell's education and experience willing to accept the job.

He had earned both his BA and MA from Howard University, a school with a history similar to Storer College. Founded just after the Civil War by a religious group to provide higher education to former slaves, Howard was also open to all willing to learn, though like Storer, attendance was primarily African American. As a student at Howard, Terrell had been immersed in college life. His experiences there helped him understand the historical role such schools had in educating African Americans, as well as the importance of higher education as a vehicle for advancement in society.

This perspective, in addition to his family's background, undoubtedly influenced his decision to accept the presidency of Storer. Terrell hailed from Duck Hill, Mississippi, a tiny town in the heart of the former Confederacy, where the horrific legacy of slavery was still fresh in the minds of many. Terrell had been born during the height of the "Jim Crow" era, in which racial segregation was enforced by a rigid set of state and local laws, and African American voting rights were often suppressed.

Through good fortune, natural ability, and hard work, Rev. Terrell left Duck Hill to pursue higher education. After Howard, he studied at Drew University Theological Seminary and later received his doctorate from New York University. An ordained Baptist minister, he served congregations in New York, New Jersey, and Florida before coming to Storer. His academic qualifications combined with an ability to lead, inspire, and manage large congregations were likely factors in his selection by the board.

Even before Rev. Terrell and his wife arrived at Storer, the Board of Trustees had to scramble to make the president's house habitable. The college was in such financial straits by that time, the Terrells had to buy their own furnishings.

Nevertheless, Rev. Terrell immediately set to work making his presence known to the staff and students, spreading the message that Storer had a lot to offer. His four main selling points were: 1) Christian interest; 2) moral values in education; 3) individual attention in a small institution; and 4) the beauty of the school's natural surroundings.

These were excellent points, but looming over them were the facts that the college still lacked full accreditation and that the cost to attend Storer was higher than nearby comparable institutions with better facilities. Given time and adequate funding, Rev. Terrell believed that the college could become competitive. The lack of adequate library space was one of the sticking points to receiving full accreditation. To that end, Rev. Terrell worked with alumni and other supporters to raise funds to build the Library Annex, which opened with great fanfare in 1953.

However, the underlying financial problems worsened, and the board actively pursued dual options to keep the college open or close it for good. Excellent plans for continuance were presented for consideration, but all required time and money, both of which were in short supply. The alumni association raised a considerable sum for the time, which helped enrollment increase for the 1954-55 school year. Yet it was not enough to sustain the college. The operating deficit continued to rise.

By all accounts, Rev. Terrell remained optimistic, rallying staff, students, alumni, and other supporters to the Storer cause. He made it a point to greet and talk with students, as noted in several oral histories. One student, Elbert Norton, told of a time when Rev. Terrell asked him to forego travelling to four away games with the basketball team. Norton was one of the star players, but he was also a member of the college *a capella* choir. The choir raised funds for the college and had an important engagement in Washington, DC, at the same time as the basketball games. After some gentle arm-twisting Norton admitted to President Terrell, "I can understand where you're coming from, and the school comes first."

In November 1954, Terrell wrote to the board, "I still have faith in Storer, in spite of everything." His optimism seemed undaunted though it was becoming clear the college could not remain open.

Five months later in April 1955, Rev. Terrell offered the board his resignation at their annual meeting. At this same meeting, the board learned that the meager annual appropriation from the state would end because of the Supreme Court's decision in *Brown v. Board of Education,* which declared it unconstitutional to establish separate schools for black and white students. This ruling meant African Americans would at least be able to apply to any school of their choosing.

Unable to see any immediate solution to the funding problem, the board voted to suspend operations for the 1955-56 school year and accept Rev. Terrell's resignation. The board and alumni still sought ways to reopen the school, but it was a futile endeavor.

After leaving Storer, Rev. Terrell continued in academia, becoming Professor of Philosophy and Religion at what was then known as Virginia State College in Petersburg, Virginia. He later became Dean of the Chapel at Howard University in Washington, DC. He died in 1988 at the age of eighty-two.

CHAPTER 25

To Preserve This Sacred Shrine

By Eugene L. Meyer

In 1954, the Supreme Court of the United States awarded a powerful victory to civil rights advocates, declaring the longstanding practice of separate schools for black and white students unconstitutional. While *Brown v. Board of Education* is often championed as a success, desegregation also sounded the death knell for many black institutions that had sprung up specifically because of racially exclusionary policies elsewhere. In this epic struggle, Storer College was collateral damage.

Following the Second World War, Storer seemed to be flourishing, if not flush. In 1948, it boasted 220 students from seventeen states, the District of Columbia, and Africa. The year before the momentous ruling in *Brown v. Board of Education*, the small college on Camp Hill, sited 400 feet above the junction of the Shenandoah and Potomac Rivers in Harpers Ferry, had celebrated its 86th anniversary. The main speaker at the event was William H. Ansel, Jr., West Virginia's state treasurer. The choice seemed fitting, as the state subsidy had sustained the school throughout much of its history.

Storer, funded initially with a grant from John Storer, a philanthropist from Maine, was open to all races but designed especially to serve African American students. Managed by Freewill Baptist missionaries, it was never a fully self-supporting "public" college. During the era of segregation, West Virginia nonetheless contributed annually in an effort to provide "separate but equal" opportunities for students of color. In later years, the state's annual subsidy ranged from $20,000 to $30,000.

Storer was never over-enrolled and enjoyed no large endowment to cushion

STORER
COLLEGE

COLLEGE GATE

A Sacred Shrine

Preserve It!

Alumni and staff attempted to stave off closing the college by making a nationwide appeal for funds. (Pamphlet courtesy of Gene Meyer)

its financial ups and downs. When West Virginia ended its segregation standard and, consequentially, its support for Storer College, it left the school on the hill standing on shaky ground.

Not everyone blamed integration and the lack of state subsidy. In a letter to the *Baltimore Sun*, Mary P. Dyson, an alumna and trustee, said these factors made "maintenance more difficult but not impossible." She alleged that the "real cause is the maladministration of the affairs of the school," indeed "astounding maladministration during the last several years." She cited "excessive student indebtedness" as "a minor example of this maladministration."

Still, almost immediately after the Supreme Court decision, the trustees voted to close the school for a year. Alumni swiftly launched a $250,000 "Save Storer Campaign," with a six-month goal of $25,000. Twelve alumni chapters pledged to raise $1,000 each. A separate foundation gave $5,000, to underwrite $100 scholarships for West Virginia students.

This surge of alumni interest buoyed Storer's president, Rev. Leonard E. Terrell. On June 9, 1954—just a little over a month after *Brown v. Board of Education* made desegregation the law of the land—the school of 100 students held its commencement exercises. Seventeen bachelor degrees were awarded. With several new white students and four new staff added to the rolls, the school reopened in the fall.

By the spring of 1955, however, the state had officially withdrawn its annual appropriation. The trustees announced that Storer, with a $46,000 deficit, would have to close. Students, alumni, and friends of the school picketed the meeting, to no avail. Eleven faculty members were dismissed. Diplomas were awarded to six students and the remaining eighty-two were urged to find other colleges. Other institutions, such as Virginia Union, pledged to welcome Storer students who wished to finish their education.

Discouraged but not deterred, Storer alumni and friends mounted another effort to reopen the school by September 1958. All that was needed, organizers said, was an initial $100,000 to renovate the school's eight major buildings. "In these days when there aren't enough facilities to go around, to keep Storer closed is a tragedy," George W. Fleming, chairman of the Washington, DC, fundraising drive, told the *Washington Post*. A fundraising brochure carried this urgent message: "Storer College – A Sacred Shrine – Preserve It."

Nannie Helen Burroughs, the prominent African American educator, civil rights activist, businesswoman, suffragette, and orator, wrote that Storer

[Has] a sacred past and it can have a glorious future.... It should remain progressive in its program and a sacred shrine in atmosphere. Storer has cost too much in willing sacrifice, in sweat and blood and tears, and produced too much in educational and religious values not to be renewed and preserved.... I do not believe 14 million colored Americans will sit by and discredit, by their indifference, the deep and moving meaning and value of an institution that means so much to both races.

In looking for ways to reopen or otherwise dispose of Storer, the trustees solicited offers from schools and charitable institutions. The A.M.E. Zion Church tendered one proposal, under which the school's name would be retained, the church would underwrite its full operation, and four of the twenty-five trustees on the new board would be from Storer. Alderson-Broaddus College, a white Baptist institution in Philippi, West Virginia, made an offer as well. On January 10, 1959, the trustees voted for the Alderson-Broaddus proposal. Under the plan, Storer's endowment of $93,000, the school's archives, and other records would be transferred to Alderson-Broaddus, which promised to earmark scholarships for black students.

Alumni and officials disagreed over this course of action. In 1959, two trustees—Madison Briscoe and Mary P. Dyson—sought to block the transfer by filing an injunction in U.S. District Court. Losing at trial, they appealed to a higher court. The protesting alumni had preferred the A.M.E. proposal, which, they said in a court filing, "lends hope and restoration...in the future operation of said Storer College."

Ultimately, a settlement was reached, with Storer's endowment and archives going to Virginia Union University, a historically black institution in Richmond. Virginia Union had been formed in 1899 from the merger of two other schools, both established, like Storer, for people of color at the close of the Civil War. What funds remained in Storer's account would be split between the Baptist-affiliated schools of Alderson-Broaddus and Virginia Union.

The settlement was facilitated by the federal government's agreement in 1962 to purchase Storer's land and nine buildings for some $200,000 to expand the Harpers Ferry National Monument. Under the agreement, the widow of Henry T. McDonald, Storer's last white president and a sometimes controversial figure, was allowed to live out her years in a house on the campus.

In 1962, Storer alumni donated $7,000 to Shepherd College, in Shepherdstown, West Virginia. This was in recognition, explained Storer Alumni President Weldon C. Malone, of the white school's acceptance of many black students and also of the many donations Storer had received from whites over the years. "Now the shoe's on the other foot," Malone was quoted as saying. "We've got to start doing some of the things that white people have been doing for us."

In 1964, Storer's main building, Anthony Memorial Hall, became the Stephen T. Mather Training Center of the National Park Service, named for the industrialist and conservationist who served as first director of the NPS, a post he held from 1916 to 1929. Today, the little school on the hill continues to be a center of learning, as National Park Service staff travel here from around the nation to further their own professional education.

In 1963, the expanded national monument at Harpers Ferry officially became Harpers Ferry National Historical Park. As custodian of Storer College, with its historic buildings, stunning views, and rich history, today's park strives to uncover, preserve, and share the stories of the place. The tales are many: some public, some personal, and all of them powerful.

Storer College gates on a foggy morning in October 2013. The campus, now preserved and protected by the National Park Service, is part of Harpers Ferry National Historical Park. (Photo courtesy of Jim Madden)

Through these gates they have passed,
    To understand,
    To connect,
    To believe,
    To enjoy,
    To learn,
    To grow,
    To love,
    To play,
    To hope,
    and
    Through these gates they will pass again.

—James Koenig

Storer College Timeline

1864-65 Julia Mann teaches refugee slaves in the Lockwood House.

Oct. 1865 30,000 newly freed African Americans reside in the Shenandoah Valley who have not yet learned to read and write.

Nov. 1865 Reverend Nathan C. Brackett arrives in Harpers Ferry as a missionary. Associated with the Freewill Baptist Home Missionary Society, he hopes to start a school in Harpers Ferry.

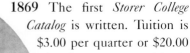

Louise V. Hicks, class of 1906.

Dec. 1865 Rev. Brackett is successful in his endeavor. The school begins in the Lockwood House with a class of 19 students. He becomes the first principal.

1866 The question is raised about establishment of a Normal School to train teachers.

Feb. 1867 John Storer, a philanthropist from Maine, agrees to donate $10,000 to the school. He stipulates that the school be open to male and female, and to black and white.

Oct. 2, 1867 Storer Normal School starts.

Mar. 1868 Storer College is granted a charter by the State of West Virginia.

1868 Lincoln Hall is erected as a dormitory for young men.

1869 The first *Storer College Catalog* is written. Tuition is $3.00 per quarter or $20.00 for five years payable in advance. Room rent was $3.00 per quarter and board $2.00 or $3.00 per week.

1875 Lura Brackett is the first teacher funded by the Free Baptist Woman's Mission Society.

May 30, 1878 The cornerstone for Myrtle Hall, later known as Mosher Hall, is laid. The building, a girls' dormitory, is dedicated on the same date the following year.

1881 Coralie Franklin, funded by the Free Baptist Woman's Mission Society, is

John Brown's Fort Museum.

Students and faculty pose in front of Lincoln Hall in this ca. 1912 postcard.

the first African American female teacher at Storer.

May 30, 1881 Frederick Douglass, one of the first trustees of the college, gives a speech praising John Brown. Proceeds from the sale of this published speech were to be used towards the endowment of a John Brown Professorship. This same day, a cornerstone of Anthony Memorial Hall is laid.

May 30, 1882 Anthony Memorial Hall, the main administration building, is dedicated.

1891 DeWolfe Industrial Building is dedicated.

1894 The Curtis Freewill Baptist Church is dedicated. It is named in honor of Rev. Silas P. Curtis.

May 26, 1897 Rev. Brackett resigns and becomes treasurer. Rev. E. E. Osgood is elected principal.

1899 Rev. Osgood resigns and Professor Henry T. McDonald is selected as president.

1903 The Lewis W. Anthony Building is erected.

1906 The Niagara Movement meets at Storer. W. E. B. Du Bois and 148 other civil rights crusaders demand equality and blaze a trail for the NAACP.

1909 The College President's house is built.

1909 Old Lincoln Hall burns.

1909 John Brown's Fort is moved and erected on cam-

William D. Johnson, class of 1904.

The College President's House.

pus. It will eventually be used as a museum and gift shop.

1911 The new Lincoln Hall is erected and renamed Brackett Hall.

1921 A Junior College degree is added to the curriculum offered at Storer College.

1927 A fire destroys much of Anthony Memorial Hall.

1938 A Women's Commission is organized.

1938 A four-year degree is added.

1940 Permelia Eastman Cook Hall is erected.

1942 75th Anniversary of Storer College.

1944 President Henry T. McDonald retires. Dr. Richard I. McKinney is selected

Storer students, ca. 1916.

Storer students on campus.

Students pose in front of Anthony Memorial Hall ca. 1923.

as president of the college and the first African American to hold the title.

1947 The Science Building is erected.

1950 Dr. McKinney resigns. Dean Le-Roy Johnson is acting president 1950-1952.

1952 Rev. Leonard Terrell is selected as last president of Storer College.

June 1955 Storer College closes after the State of West Virginia drops its funding, a result of the U.S. Supreme Court Case, *Brown v. Board of Education* that ended segregation. Low enrollment and financial strain contributed to the decision to close.

Student Jesse Bradford (left) in cooking class.

Contributors

James Beckman is currently a Professor of Legal Studies at the University of Central Florida and loves reading and writing about Harpers Ferry in his spare time. He was an artist-in-residence at the Park in 2001 and has written a book about Harpers Ferry (*Harpers Ferry*, Arcadia, 2006), as well as other articles on John Brown, Storer College, and Jefferson County history. He lives part of the year in Bolivar/Harpers Ferry and has fallen in love with the area and its rich history.

George Best has worked for both Harpers Ferry National Historical Park and the Harpers Ferry Park Association in various capacities since 2010. He is a graduate of Centre College and James Madison University, where he earned a bachelor's degree in history and a master's degree in American history, respectively.

Todd Bolton began working for the National Park Service in 1977 and currently serves as Chief of Visitor Services at Harpers Ferry National Historical Park. He has a B.S. in park administration from Shepherd University and has been involved in African American history research for over thirty-five years.

Dawne Raines Burke, PhD, is an award-winning professor of Education and Human Development at Shepherd University. She holds degrees from Virginia Polytechnic Institute and State University, as well as Shepherd University. She has authored several scholarly articles and a book, *An American Phoenix: The History of Storer College from Slavery to Desegregation, 1865-1955 (Commemorative Edition)*. She has also collaborated on a number of documentary film projects concerning Storer College and Harpers Ferry.

Matt Coletti is a professional historian with History Associates, Inc. Mr. Coletti holds a B.A. in history from Washington College (Chestertown, Maryland), and a joint MA in history and public history from the University of Massachusetts–Amherst. While the number of research projects Mr. Coletti pursues are diverse, his historical interests primarily lie in American historical memory, the American Civil War, and general postwar commemorative practices.

Autumn H. Cook is the web manager and social media specialist at Harpers Ferry National Historical Park. She has worked at the park in some capacity since 2004, and eight years of her career were devoted to teaching both local and visiting students. She loves to conduct research and credits her MLIS degree for equipping her with the skillset to find answers to the most challenging research inquiries.

Emma Dacol holds a bachelor's degree in biology from Goucher College and is pursuing a Master's of Fine Arts degree in film and electronic media at American University. Her films have screened at festivals and on Maryland Public Television, and include *Garbology* (2016), *The Monarch Butterfly Effect* (2015), *Vanishing Vistas: Preserving Catoctin's Scenic Vistas in a Changing Climate* (2015), *Chesapeake Villages* (2014), and *The Most Endangered Species in the Bay: The Waterman* (2013). She is currently producing a short documentary film about Dr. Madison Spencer Briscoe, a Storer College alumnus and professor.

Melinda Day has been a park ranger with Harpers Ferry National Historical Park since the early 1980s, working in the park's living history branch. She enjoys offering public history programs utilizing the park's vast array of material culture and decorative arts as historic settings for visitors to engage multiple perspectives of the town's former inhabitants.

David Fox has served Harpers Ferry National Historical Park since 1989. Arriving as environmentalist, he got bit by the "history bug" and has been consumed by the history of Harpers Ferry ever since. Although he is a park ranger, he considers his primary job interpretation and strives to impart the story of Harpers Ferry in a manner that captivates and involves all visitors.

James F. Horn graduated from Shepherd University in May of 2014 with a degree in history and a concentration in the Civil War and nineteenth century America. Horn worked at Harpers Ferry National Historical Park for three years, and today works as a seasonal park ranger at Cedar Creek and Belle Grove National Historical Park. Horn is also the author of *World War I and Jefferson County, West Virginia* (The History Press, 2017)

James Koenig earned his BA in history from the University of Maryland–Baltimore County, and his MA in museum studies at the Cooperstown Graduate Programs. He is a volunteer at Harpers Ferry National Historical Park and was Volunteer of the Year for the National Capital Region in 2006. Jim has won numerous writing awards and has been published in several anthologies of Appalachian and West Virginia writers.

John Lustrea received a master's degree in public history with a concentration in museum studies from the University of South Carolina in Columbia in May 2017. He worked at Harpers Ferry National Historical Park for four summers (2012-2016) as an interpretive ranger.

James P. Madden and his wife Loretta have been VIP (Volunteers in Park) every October since their first visit in 2009. Jim credits his early interest in Harpers Ferry and the Civil War to his sixth grade Kansas history class, in which he studied John Brown's roles in "Bloody Kansas" and the later capture of the Harpers Ferry armory. He enjoys not only the daily contact with visitors to the park, but also researching some of the unanswered questions that still linger about the history of Harpers Ferry.

Jim, a graduate of Kansas State University, is still active as a real estate broker in Fort Collins, Colorado, while Loretta is a retired teacher.

Eugene L. Meyer, a veteran journalist and author, is writing a book about the five African American raiders who accompanied John Brown at Harpers Ferry in 1859. The book *Five for Freedom* is scheduled to be published in early 2018 by Lawrence Hill Books, an imprint of Chicago Review Press.

Connie Park Rice, PhD, is a lecturer of history at West Virginia University, where she also earned her bachelor's, master's, and doctoral degrees in history. She is assistant editor of *West Virginia History: A Journal of Regional Studies* and is a member of the Governor's West Virginia Sesquicentennial of the American Civil War Commission. Her work has been published in a number of scholarly journals and anthologies. Her current projects include a biography of civil rights pioneer J. R. Clifford, and research of Black political activity in West Virginia following emancipation.

John M. Rudy is a National Park Service ranger and interpretive trainer with the Interpretive Development Program at Mather Training Center in Harpers Ferry. He holds a BA in history from Gettysburg College and an MA in applied history from Shippensburg University. He lives in Gettysburg, Pennsylvania.

Creighton Waters is a native of Martinsburg, West Virginia. He is a graduate of Shepherd University, where he earned BA degrees in park administration and history. He has been employed at Harpers Ferry National Historical Park as an interpretive park ranger since 1990. Creighton is married to Betsy Waters and has one son, Samuel.

Sarah White grew up in Martinsburg, West Virginia. She graduated from West Virginia University in 2016 with a degree in medical lab science with a concentration in histotechnology. She spent four summers working for the National Park Service, three of those being in Harpers Ferry. Her experience with the NPS gave her a deeper appreciation for history.

Eugene Wilkins, a Texas native and retiree, has served with his wife, Lennie, as Volunteers in Park for the past eighteen years. Their volunteerism has included stints at Harpers Ferry, as well as Apostle Islands National Lakeshore (Wisconsin), Joshua Tree National Park (California), Pictured Rocks National Lakeshore (Michigan), Prince William Forest National Park (Virginia), and Redwoods National Park (California). Wilkins collaborated with his daughter Wil (also a volunteer) on the article, "Washington's Last War, Harpers Ferry's First," published in the *Magazine of the Jefferson County Historical Society*, Charles Town, West Virginia, December 2010.

Selected Bibliography

This is a partial list of sources used for the research of this book. Many were accessed by more than one contributing author. Those seeking further research, citations, or material related to these chapters can contact Harpers Ferry National Historical Park or the Harpers Ferry Park Association.

Books

Anthony, Kate J. *Storer College, Harper's Ferry, W. VA: A Brief Historical Sketch with Supplementary Notes, 1867-1891*. Boston, MA: Morning Star Publishing House, 1891.

Anthony, Susan B. and Ida Husted Harper. *The History of Woman Suffrage*. Vol. 4. Hollenbeck Press, 1902.

Barry, Joseph, Jr. *The Annals of Harper's Ferry: From the Establishment of the National Armory in 1794, to the Present Time, 1869*. Hagerstown, MD: Dechert & Company Printers, 1869.

Briscoe, Madison, S. *A Laboratory Manual for General Biology*. Harpers Ferry, WV, 1934.

———. *Natural History Checklist of the Harpers Ferry Area*. Harpers Ferry, WV, 1935.

Burgess, Gideon A. and John T. Ward. *Free Baptist Cyclopaedia*. Chicago, IL: The Woman's Temperance Publication Association, 1889.

Burke, Dawne Raines. *An American Phoenix: A History of Storer College from Slavery to Desegregation, 1865-1955*. Pittsburgh, PA: Geyer Printing, 2006.

Burlingame-Cheney, Emeline. *The Story of the Life and Work of Oren B. Cheney: Founder and First President of Bates College*. Boston, MA: Morning Star Publishing House, 1907.

Burrage, Henry S. *History of the Baptists in Maine*. Portland, ME: Marks Printing House, 1904.

Caldwell, A. B. *History of the American Negro: West Virginia Edition*. Vol. VII. Atlanta, GA: A. B. Caldwell Pub. Co., 1923.

Davis, Mary A. *History of the Free Baptist Woman's Missionary Society*. Boston, MA: Morning Star Publishing House, 1900.

Douglass, Frederick. *"John Brown: An Address by Frederick Douglass at the Fourteenth Anniversary of Storer College Harper's Ferry, West Virginia, May 30, 1881."* Dover, NH: Morning Star Job Printing House, 1881.

Drumgoold, Kate. *A Slave Girl's Story: Being an Autobiography of Kate Drumgoold*. Brooklyn, 1898.

Du Bois, William Edward Burghardt. *The Souls of Black Folk*. Mineola, NY: Dover Publications, Thrift Editions, 1994.

Emery, Edwin. *The History of Sanford, Maine, 1661–1900*. Fall River, MA: Published by the Compiler, 1901.

Etter-Lewis, Gwen and Richard W. Thomas, eds. *Lights of the Spirit: Historical Portraits of Black Baha'is in North America: 1898-2000*. Wilmette, IL: Baha'i Publishing Trust, 2006.

Flemming, G. James and, Christian E. Burckel. *Who's Who in Colored America*. Yonkers-on-Hudson, NY: Christian E. Burckel & Associates, 1950.

Foner, Eric. *Reconstruction: America's Unfinished Revolution, 1863-1877*. 1st Ed. New York: First Perennial Classics, 2002.

The Free Baptist Woman's Missionary Society, 1873-1921. Providence, RI: The Society, 1922.

Hadlock, Richard. *Jazz Masters of the Twenties*. New York: The Macmillan Company, 1988.

Hahn, Steven. *A Nation Under Our Feet: Black Political Struggles in the Rural South from Slavery to the Great Migration*. Cambridge: Harvard University, 2003.

Humbert, Judy, and June Gaskins-Davis. *History of Douglas School Winchester, VA: A Tribute to Endurance, Belief, Perseverance, and Success*. Winchester, VA: Winchester-Frederick County Historical Society, 2014.

John Brown's Raid, National Park Service History Series. Harpers Ferry, WV: Harpers Ferry Historical Association, 2009.

Kennedy-Nolle, Sharon D. *Writing Reconstruction: Race, Gender, and Citizenship in the Postwar South*. Chapel Hill: University of North Carolina Press, 2015.

Lewis, Ralph. *An Historical Sketch of Camp Hill-Wesley Methodist Church*. Harpers Ferry, WV: Harpers Ferry Historical Association, 1996.

Maury, M. F. and W. M. Fontaine. *Resources of West Virginia*. Wheeling, WV: Register Company, 1876.

Miller, Thomas Condit, and Hu Maxwell. *West Virginia and Its People*. Vol. III. New York, NY: Lewis Historical Publishing, 1913.

Morgan, Benjamin S. and J. F. Cork. *History of Education in West Virginia*. Charleston, WV: Moses W. Donnally, 1893.

Moyer, Teresa S., and Paul A. Shackel. *The Making of Harpers Ferry National Historical Park; A Devil, Two Rivers, and a Dream*. Lanham, MD: AltaMira Press, 2008.

Parker, Kathryn. *Images of America: Winchester*. Charleston, SC: Arcadia Publishing, 2006.

Quarles, Benjamin. *Allies for Freedom: Blacks and John Brown.* New York: Oxford University Press, 1974.

Quarles, Garland R. *The Story of One Hundred Old Homes in Winchester, Virginia.* Winchester, VA: Winchester-Frederick County Historical Society, 1993.

Reilly, Wayne E., ed. *Sarah Jane Foster: Teacher of the Freedmen, a Diary and Letters.* Charlottesville: The University Press of Virginia, 1990.

Richards, E. S. *The Tiger: New Orleans University 1928 Yearbook.* New Orleans: A.W. Hyatt Stationery Mfg. Co., 1928.

Rosenkrantz, Timme. *Harlem Jazz Adventures: A European Baron's Memoir, 1934-1969.* Scarecrow Press, 2012.

Shaw, Arnold. *The Jazz Age: Popular Music in the 1920s.* Oxford University Press, 1989.

Stetson, W. W. and B. A. Hinsdale. *History and Civil Government of Maine.* Chicago, IL: Werner School Book Company, 1898.

Taylor, Julius H., Clyde R. Dillard, Nathaniel K. Proctor, and Herman R. Branson. *The Negro in Science.* Baltimore, MD: Morgan State College Press, 1955

Toogood, Anna Coxe. *The Lockwood House: Birthplace of Storer College.* Washington, DC: U.S. Office of Archeology and Historic Preservation, 1969.

Articles, Blogs, Chapters, Dissertations, Reports

Ames, Mary Clemmer. "Yankee Teachers in the Valley of Virginia." *The Independent,* December 1866.

Barnett, Anthony, Armin Büttner, Leif Bo Petersen, Howard Rye, Mario Schneeberger and Dieter Salemann Compilers. "Don Redman's 1946 European Tour," February 2013. https://donredman1946tour.wordpress.com.

Beckman, James. "Storer College and African American Home Ownership in Jefferson County." *Magazine of the Jefferson County Historical Society,* Vol. LXX (December 2004): pp. 80-89.

"Bluefield State College Presidents: Principal Hamilton Hatter 1895-1906." Bluefield State College Archives. http://www.bluefieldstate.edu/archives/website/hatter.htm5

Brackett, Rev. Nathan C. "Biographical Sketch of the Rev. A. H. Morrell." (Reprinted from *The Morning Star,* February 27, 1886, with slight difference.)

Brewster, Rev. J. M. "Who Was John Storer?" *The Missionary Helper.* Vol. VI, (February 1882): pp. 234-235. (Excerpted from *The Morning Star,* February 1882)

Briscoe, Madison, S. "Some Ecological Aspects of Liberia as Interpreted from the Vegetation on Ground and Aerial Photography with Special Reference to the Distribution of Parasites." PhD diss., The Catholic University of America, 1950.

Burke, Dawne Raines. "Nnamdi's Journey, Part I and Part II." *Shepherdstown Good News Paper*, Summer and Fall, 2003.

———. "Storer College: A Hope for Redemption in the Shadow of Slavery, 1865-1955," PhD diss., Virginia Polytechnic Institute & State College, 2004.

Callahan, James Morton. *History of West Virginia, Old and New, and West Virginia Biography*. Vol. II. Chicago: The American Historical Society, 1923.

Chatafrik Network. "Biography of Nnamdi Azikiwe." May 8, 2012. chatafrik.com/special/spotlight/biography/biography-of-nnamdi-azikiwe#.WXsT68eGPIV

Cheney, Oren B. Freewill Baptist Correspondence to N. C. Brackett, March 15, 1867. West Virginia Collection, Wise Library, West Virginia University: A&M 1322.

Clifford, John R. "Annual Address to the National Independent Political League," *Pioneer Press*, September 2, 1911.

———. "You Can, Then Why Not be a Good Reader?" *Pioneer Press*, September 1886.

Copy of the Records of the Bureau of Refugees, Freedmen, and Abandoned Lands. RG 105. Harpers Ferry National Historical Park Archives and Library, Harpers Ferry, WV.

Cromwell, John W. "Communications." Letter to the editor. *Journal of Negro History*, Vol. 8, No. 3 (July 1923): pp. 339-340.

Curtis Freewill Baptist Church Ledger, Harpers Ferry National Historical Park Museum Collection, Catalog #HAFE 238321. Harpers Ferry National Historical Park Archives and Library, Harpers Ferry, WV.

Daniel, Allen Mercer. "The Lovetts of Harpers Ferry, West Virginia." *Negro History Bulletin*. Vol. 32 (February, 1969): pp. 14-19.

Driggs, Frank. "Don Redman, Jazz Composer Arranger." *The Jazz Review*. Vol. 2, No. 10, (November 1959).

Eff, Elaine. "Storer College Oral History Project, HAFE." Interviews with former Storer College students, 2014. Harpers Ferry National Historical Park Archives and Library, Harpers Ferry, WV.

Fairbairn, Charlotte J. "John Brown's Fort (Armory and Guard House), Historic Structures Report Part I, Historical Data Section." August 15, 1961, HSR-202. Harpers Ferry National Historical Park Archives and Library, Harpers Ferry, WV.

Gee, Clarence S. "John Brown's Fort." *West Virginia History*. Vol. 19, No. 2 (January 1958): pp. 93-100.

Gerard, Jim. "Don Redman: Setting the Template." *All About Jazz*, May 29, 2012. www.allaboutjazz.com/don-redman-setting-the-template-don-redman-by-jim-gerard.php?width=1024.

Gozdzik, Gloria. "A Historical Resource Study for Storer College Harpers Ferry, West Virginia." Horizon Research Consultants Report, January 2002.

"Hamilton Hatter." West Virginia Division of Culture and History. 2015. http://www.wvculture.org/history/histamne/hatter.html

Johnson, Mary. "An 'Ever Present Bone of Contention': The Heyward Shepherd Memorial." *West Virginia History*. Vol. 56. (1997): pp. 1-26.

———. "Package 119, Park Building 56 (Lockwood House), 57 (Brackett House), and 58 (Morrell House), Harpers Ferry National Historical Park, 1796-1962." Historic structures report for the National Park Service and University of Maryland Cooperative Agreement, 1995. Harpers Ferry National Historical Park Archives and Library, Harpers Ferry, WV.

Kahrl, Andrew. "The Political Work of Leisure: Class, Recreation, and African American Commemoration at Harpers Ferry, West Virginia, 1881-1931." *Journal of Social History*. Vol. 42, No. 1 (Fall 2008): pp. 57-77.

Kwekudee. "Nnamdi Azikiwe: The Great Pan-Africanist and First President of Nigeria." *Trip Down Memory Lane*, June 21, 2013, https://kwekudee-tripdownmemorylane.blogspot.com/2013/06/nnamdi-aziki-we-great-pan-africanist-and.html.

Maine State Seminary Catalogue, 1866 and 1867. Freewill Baptist Collection, Muskie Archives, Bates College, Lewiston, ME.

McClain, Mary Ellen. "Storer College: Harper's Ferry, West Virginia (1865 - 1897)." Honors History Thesis. Linfield College, McMinnville, OR, April 15, 1974.

McDonald, Henry T. "The Home Mission School: The Young People's Topic." Harpers Ferry National Historical Park Archives and Library, Harpers Ferry, WV.

———. "Storer College." *History of Education in West Virginia*. Charleston, WV: The Tribune Printing Company, 1904.

McKinney, Richard I. Interview by T. Bolton and G. Roper in Baltimore, MD, November 30, 1988. Storer College Oral History Project. Harpers Ferry National Historical Park Archives and Library, Harpers Ferry, WV.

Meyer, Joyce D. "New Frontiers: A. Mercer Daniel (1887-1976) and the American Association of Law Libraries." American Association of Law Libraries Archives, University of Illinois Archives, 2009.

The Missionary Helper. Vols. 1 though IX, 1878-1886. Boston, MA: Free Baptist Woman's Missionary Society.

The Missionary Helper. Supplemental issues, Annual Reports of the Free Baptist Woman's Missionary Society, Presented at Annual Meetings, 1880-1885. Boston, MA: Free Baptist Woman's Missionary Society.

Mongin, Alfred. "A College in Secessia: The Early Years of Storer College." *West Virginia History*, Vol. 23, No. 4 (July 1962): p. 2.

Morrell, Alexander H., Rev., "The Morrell Diary." Chepachet Baptist Church, 2017. http://www.chepachetbaptist.org/morrelldiary1.htm

National Park Service. "Curtis Freewill Baptist Church." Historic American Building Survey, HABS No. WV-27.

National Park Service. "Morrell House." Historic American Building Survey, HABS no. WV-171.

National Park Service. "Paymaster's Quarters (Lockwood House)." Historic American Building Survey, HABS No. WV-179.

O'Donnell, Patricia M., Carrie A. Mardorf, and Sarah L. Graulty. "Camp Hill Cultural Landscape Report, Harpers Ferry National Historical Park, Harpers Ferry, WV, Project No: HAFE 041186." Prepared by Heritage Landscapes, LLC for the National Park Service, June 2009. Harpers Ferry National Historical Park Archives and Library, Harpers Ferry, WV.

Prillerman, Byrd. "Development of the Colored School System." *History of Education in West Virginia*. Edited by Thomas C. Miller. Charleston, WV: The Tribune Printing Company, 1904.

Rasmussen, Barbara. "Sixty-Four Edited Letters of the Founders of Storer College." Unpublished Master's Thesis. West Virginia University, Morganton, WV, 1986.

———. "Anne S. Dudley." e-WV: The West Virginia Encyclopedia. October 18, 2012. www.wvencyclopedia.org/articles/1969. Accessed, January 20, 2017.

Rice, Connie Park. "Coralie Franklin Cook." *African American National Biography*. Oxford University Press, March 2013.

Schelle, Crystal. "Storer College graduate reflects on time as student." *The Herald Mail*, February 5, 2017.

Shackel, Paul A. "Terrible Saint: Changing Meanings of the John Brown Fort," *Historical Archaeology*, Vol. 29, No. 4 (1995): pp. 11-25.

Shapiro, Stephanie. "A black college closed in 1955, but its fading alumni fight to pass on a legacy." *Washington Post Magazine*, October 22, 2015.

Smith, Linell. "Minister to the Mind." *The Baltimore Sun*, November 24, 1996.

Stealey, John Edmund III. "The Freedmen's Bureau in West Virginia." *The Magazine of the Jefferson County Historical Society*, Vol. 68 (December 2002): pp. 26-27, 33.

———. "Reports of Freedmen's Bureau Operations in West Virginia: Agents in the Eastern Panhandle." *West Virginia History*, Vol. 42 (1980-1981): pp. 101-103.

Storer, John Parker Boyd (great-grandson of John Storer). Telephone interview with Dawne Raines Burke, July 31, 2002.

Stuart, Claire. "Madison Spencer Briscoe: Renaissance Man." *Shepherdstown Good News Paper*, Summer, 2002.

Surkamp, Jim. "Jefferson County—A Profile of Prosperity." *Civil War Scholars*, June 18, 2011, http://civilwarscholars.com/2011/06/jefferson-county-1860-a-profile-of-prosperity.

Unaegbunam, Jeff. "Dr. Nnamdi Azikiwe (1904-1996): A Detailed Documentary." YouTube video. Published January 2, 2011. www.youtube.com/watch?v=2z5fQ9oaVU8.

Archives, Collections

Athletic History of Black Colleges and Universities. Dale Fulmer and Bob Grube, Personal Research Collection, June 26, 2007.

Brackett-Newcomer Papers. Harpers Ferry National Historical Park Archives and Library, Harpers Ferry, WV.

Catalogues of Storer College, published by the Board of Trustees, 1868-1955. Harpers Ferry National Historic Park Archives and Library, Harpers Ferry, WV.

Don Redman Archives. Don Redman Society, Piedmont, WV.

Du Bois, W. E. B. Papers. University of Massachusetts Amherst, Special Collections.

McDonald, Henry T. Papers. Harpers Ferry National Historical Park Archives and Library, Harpers Ferry, WV.

Storer College Alumni and Student Records. West Virginia and Regional History Center, West Virginia University Library, Morgantown, WV.

Storer College Archives. Harpers Ferry National Historic Park Archives and Library, Harpers Ferry, WV.

Storer College Digital Collection. West Virginia and Regional History Center, West Virginia University Library, Morgantown, WV.

Storer Record, 1894-1954. Harpers Ferry National Historical Park Archives and Library, Harpers Ferry, WV.

Newspapers

Baltimore Afro-American

Baltimore Sun

Cumberland Evening Times (Cumberland, MD), 1892-1916

Detroit Free Press

Evening Journal, Journal (Martinsburg, WV)

Evening Star (Washington, DC), 1854-1972

Morning Star (Maine, New Hampshire, et al), 1826-1911

New York Times

Pioneer Press (Martinsburg, WV), 1882-1917

Pittsburgh Courier (Pittsburgh, PA), 1907-1966

Shepherdstown Register (Shepherdstown, WV), 1849-1955

Spirit of Jefferson (Charles Town, VA), 1844-1948

Spirit of Jefferson: Farmers Advocate (Charles Town, VA), 1948-

Vermont Phoenix (Brattleboro, VT), 1834-1955

Virginia Free Press (Charles Town, VA), 1835-1860

Washington Herald, 1906-1939

Washington Post

Washington Times

Wheeling Daily Intelligencer (Wheeling, WV), 1865-1903

Index